£1.00 net

SIMON JOHN CARR

24 LANGLEY DRIVE

NORTON.

GEORGE BEST'S SOCCER ANNUAL

No. 5

GEORGE BEST'S SOCCER ANNUAL No. 5

PELHAM BOOKS

First published in Great Britain by
PELHAM BOOKS LTD
52 Bedford Square
London W.C.1
1972

SBN 7207 0587 8

Made and printed in Great Britain by
Fletcher & Son Ltd, Norwich

Contents

Acrobatics by Denis Law (Manchester United) come to no avail as Crystal Palace's Wall heads clear

Ken Stanley with George Best

Introduction
by Ken Stanley

How time flies. It only seems five minutes ago since I had the pleasure of introducing George's No. 2 Annual. During this three-year period, George has certainly packed in a great deal of soccer and with it all the thrills and entertainment that go with this wonderful sport.

His skills continue to delight the soccer crowds as well as the millions of television viewers and he adds glamour and excitement in every game he plays.

George is acclaimed now by all but a few as the World's No. 1 Soccer Star and I firmly believe that he will continue going forward and finally prove beyond doubt to the remaining few that he is the greatest footballer the World has ever seen.

Just as George sparkles – so does his Soccer Annual and I am sure you will agree with me that the pictures and articles in this year's Annual make it the best to date and that's saying something!

Here's wishing you, the readers, many hours of pleasure with Annual No. 5.

The Pressures on a Top Professional Footballer *by GEORGE BEST*

So this chap said to me: 'What's it like – what's it like coping with all the pressures that you top footballers have to face? I mean, it's all right for us, we just go along to watch you play. But surely you must sometimes feel that life is just too much?'

At least this chap put it rather nicely. More often than not, the fans think we players lead a nice easy life and even if the pressure does get a bit too strong sometimes – well, that's what we're paid for.

Obviously there is a lot of pressure when you get into the top flight of football. Success is all-important and we can't all be winning something, so the strain gets that much greater. What matters is how you learn to cope with the pressure. Some players, and I won't mention any names to protect them from something not their fault, do crack up.

That's apart from, say, Peter Knowles, formerly of Wolves and a good player, who just felt that the 'warfare' of modern football didn't fit in with his very strong religious principles.

I'm lucky in that I don't really suffer from nerves. I can feel perfectly relaxed before a big game, maybe chatting with mates outside the dressing-room until the very last minute. Others may be going through some superstitious ritual, and others still may be literally sick before going out through the tunnel.

At first, I wasn't aware of any special pressures. I got into the Manchester United team at seventeen, and into the Northern Ireland side around the same time. Gradually I built a bit of a name for myself and found myself hitting the headlines. It happened fast, but it didn't worry me.

But when you talk about pressures, it's obvious they get greater the higher up the ladder of soccer fame you go. There may be pressures of sheer survival if you're playing for a Fourth Division side, because a drop in gates, which usually follows a run of defeats, can mean the club going out of business.

I've played all my football as a professional with just the one club . . . United. And whether we're winning a championship or the Cup, or whether we're in the middle of a bad spell, the fact is that other clubs are always keen to beat us.

Take Everton, who won the championship a couple of years or so ago. They played well through the run-in and deserved their success. But the following season, they found the pressure had increased no end. Suddenly, as Champions, they were the target for everybody else. Even no-hopers, and there aren't

'It's a matter, I suppose, of belief in yourself . . .'

George Best signs an autograph for one of his many thousands of young fans

many in the First Division, felt they had to beat Everton as a sort of status symbol.

So actually winning something makes it that much harder to keep going. The pressure is on . . .

It's how you cope with it that matters.

For me, it's pleasing to read that my presence in a game can put a few thousand on the gate. So, naturally, the question arises: 'Do you feel extra pressure with this kind of responsibility?'

The answer has to be no. Simply because once the game has started, I'm only conscious of the play itself. I'm completely immersed in what is happening out on the park . . . not whether I personally am contributing my full share of entertainment to the man who has forked out a few bob specifically to see me play.

In fact, I contribute entertainment value on away games just by being robbed of the ball a few times. The roar of delight from opposing fans is quite something . . . I know this because our coach, Malcolm Musgrove, has talked to me about it often enough. One can imagine the mixed feelings of fans. On the one hand, they would like to see something spectacular from a

top visiting player; on the other, they like to see him rendered useless by their own players.

So as George Best, and as a part of Manchester United, I know about the pressures. I've had a fair share of criticism in my life and I've had to learn to take it. If I'm in some kind of disciplinary trouble, I know that I'm going to be hounded by journalists who, after all, are technically only doing their job.

It's up to me to keep out of their way on these occasions. Hence odd little tricks, like getting off a train a couple of stops earlier than expected, just to give myself a bit of privacy.

With the pressure goes that basic lack of privacy. The windows in my home in Cheshire are made of glass that enable me to see the scenery outside but which prevent anybody outside looking in. That's fair enough, I think – and a better ploy than lace curtains, which most other people have!

There's the lack of privacy you feel when you go out for a quiet drink or a meal. It only needs a gossip-mongering expert to get around a bit and suddenly you were raving drunk at four o'clock in the morning in

It's gone thataway! The pressure is on in a league match against Wolves. Gerry Taylor and George Best keep their eyes on the ball

some terrible little club . . . and surrounded by a bevy of beauties who most certainly weren't footballing colleagues!

But the fact is that you have to accept that most of your life is lived in a sort of goldfish bowl . . . that's if you want to survive in the top class of soccer. What has annoyed me is the way that my family back home in Belfast have sometimes been dragged into controversies.

When I missed one important Northern Ireland game in Russia, and missed it through injury, there were people who reckoned I was faking the injury because I couldn't be bothered to make the trip to Moscow. And, inevitably, I suppose they made some pretty nasty attacks on my mother, as if she was somehow responsible.

I'd like to get to meet some of the people who make these remarks – or for that matter some of the ones who send me poison-pen letters. It's not that they worry me – it's just that most of them are simply cowards who won't even come out in the open and it

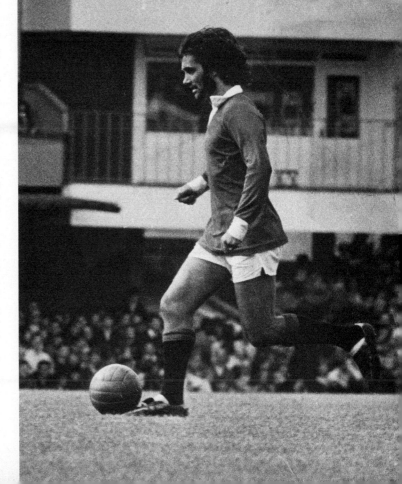

George Best heading straight for goal

The pressure was also on referees last season – as the above picture and the one on the opposite page show all too clearly

With the pressure off, George Best juggles with the ball

would give me a little pleasure to frighten them a bit.

But there's another form of pressure which is sometimes hard to live with. We're in the middle of the mass-coverage era. Television, radio, the newspapers – soccer is lived out in the spotlight all the time, and that also is inevitable because the game has become so popular and also because so much money is involved in it.

The seventeen-year-old, thrown in at the deep end in a vital FA Cup-tie – well, he's going to have every available detail about his background and beliefs splashed around all over the place. Someone like Trevor Francis, only sixteen when he started banging in goals galore for Birmingham City, became a celebrity to such an extent that even maiden aunts knew all about him.

You have got to have a pretty strong character to be able to take all that – and not start believing entirely in your own publicity. And you've got to learn that you must take knocks off the pitch as well as on it.

One thinks of the 'little' incidents that crop up from time to time in football – the star player 'caught' out of bounds before a big game, that kind of thing. He's lucky if that indiscretion doesn't force the world economic situation off the front page of the newspapers!

Another aspect of the pressure is that I find I'm asked to answer queries on things like politics (a specially hot subject where I come from) and religion and what the well-dressed girl should be wearing. So I say what I think, trying to be helpful.

And then find that another newspaper reckons they're fed up with me talking about anything but soccer and nominating me as 'Bore Of The Year'!

Sometimes you feel you just can't win. But it's the ability to cope with these pressures that matters. I can't repeat that often enough.

And the actual pressures out there on the field of play? The bigger your reputation, the more determined any defender is to make you look stupid. You have to have the confidence to make him look a mug if possible. You have to realize that he's not having a go at you personally, just the threat that you carry to his team.

As I said earlier, I've been blessed with the sort of personality that can cope with pressures – mainly because I don't have nerves. Well, not often . . .

But that's not to deny the fact that the pressures at

Above: *General salute. The crowd acclaim a George Best goal as he waves back*
Below: *George takes to the air in a league match against Wolves at Old Trafford*

the top are greater today than they have ever been. If I'm lucky, then be sure that many players find the strain and stress just about too much.

It's a matter, I suppose, of belief in yourself and your ability to fight back.

Somebody once wrote of me that I was a 'living James Dean – a rebel with a cause. The cause of his club and country'.

I don't mind that quote at all. Even if living up to it does add a bit more pressure in the pressure-cooker in which I live, play, sleep and breathe.

In line of duty. Blythe (Crystal Palace) heads clear of Manchester United's George Best

My Travels in the ....Football World.............

by GORDON BANKS

One of the bonuses about being a professional footballer is that you meet all kinds of people and travel to many places which, otherwise, would be simply names on a map to you. For top-class soccer means football around the world, these days.

I wonder if you've any idea how many countries some professional footballers see, during their careers with their clubs and – if they make the highest grade – their countries? I'll save you playing a guessing game, and tell you that I've visited around two dozen countries, during my time with Leicester City, Stoke City and England.

France, Holland, Belgium, East Germany, West Germany, Norway, Denmark and Sweden, Portugal, Spain, Italy, Switzerland, Yugoslavia, Czechoslovakia, Poland, Greece, South Africa, Uruguay, Brazil, Mexico . . . I've been to all of these countries, staying at top-class hotels, playing on the grounds of world-famous stadiums.

Oh, yes . . . and I've also been to Malta, not to mention Scotland, Ireland and Wales!

Two World Cup tournaments mean that as well as having played in the Final at Wembley in 1966, I travelled to Mexico for the 1970 competition. I was also an England reserve in the 1962 tournament, which was played in Chile, but as England took only two goalkeepers with them on that trip, I stayed home on stand-by as it were.

My soccer travels have certainly provided me with memories to last a lifetime, if I never go abroad again. And probably the highlight – apart from having won a World Cup winner's medal at Wembley in 1966 – was when I went to Brazil, and played in the fabulous Maracana stadium there. This magnificent ground can hold 200,000 people.

When I played there, it wasn't quite a capacity crowd – there were 150,000 people inside the stadium – but it looked pretty well packed, and the atmosphere was terrific.

Around the pitch there is a moat, and when you see the stadium illuminated by the floodlights, and the flags flying, and the throng of fans setting off fire-crackers, you realize that football in Brazil is more than just a national sport . . . it's almost a religion.

The dressing-rooms are fabulous: they're underneath the ground, and I reckon that there must be billions of two-inch tiles on the walls and floors of the vast area. The size of one dressing-room alone must be as big as our gymnasium at Stoke. And there's a bath for each player!

I got my first close-up of Brazil in the 'little World

really be described as football pitches – there was some grass, but the ground was rutted, as if by the marks of cart tracks. Yet these Brazilian boys were playing, bare-footed, and doing tricks with the ball that had even seasoned professional players staring.

I know when I was in Brazil, I received a surprise or two about the progress that had been made in the

The hands have it! Gordon Banks shows the safest pair of hands in English football . . .
and that's the size they often look to opposing forwards

Cup' of 1965, and I can tell you that out there, all the kids are absolutely soccer-mad. It's not surprising, when you consider that for many of them, soccer stardom means an escape from poverty. It really is 'rags to riches'.

I can remember Ronnie Clayton, who was at one time the skipper of England, as well as of Blackburn Rovers, saying how he had been impressed by the way the youngsters learned their football in Brazil. Ronnie had seen them playing on surfaces which could not

game there. We stayed at an hotel which was close to the beach, and there was a sort of dual carriageway running along, with patches of bare land near by.

The ground was baked hard, and very bumpy, yet I was very much struck by the wonderful way the youngsters playing soccer on these patches of land could control a football.

Three years ago, I was out there again, and we stayed at the same hotel where we had been before. When we looked out from our rooms, we could see that

18

all the bumpy ground had been flattened and scraped until it was absolutely level. Not only that – it had all been converted, until there must have been between twenty and thirty little football pitches, for games of seven or eight a side. The surface was still bare and dusty, but floodlights had been erected. We arrived there fairly late in the evening, and when we had had a meal and unpacked, we went out for a stroll. It was about 11.30 at night, by that time, and it really was an amazing sight which met our eyes, as we walked along.

Every single one of these little pitches was illuminated by the floodlights . . . and on every single one of the grounds there was a game going on. Yes, at nearly midnight! Can you imagine the scene . . . twenty or thirty games being played, under the lights, for almost as far as the eye could see – and at that time of the night!

Of course, it's the ambition of every Brazilian kid to become the new Pele. Brazil's 'Black Pearl', who recently retired from international competition, although he'll continue to play for Santos for another year or so, has really become an idol and a figure to be emulated in his country.

Pele is reputed to have made a fortune from his uncanny ability to play football and mesmerize opponents. He has made a great deal of money from the

'It's the ambition of every Brazilian kid to become a new Pele'

Gordon Banks (centre) *with some of the England players in Mexico, 1970*

game itself; and outside soccer there are all sorts of things which have added to his earnings. If I remember correctly, there was even a coffee named after him.

So those Brazilian youngsters have seen what soccer can do for someone; they have seen that it's a game which can bring fame and fortune. And they're fanatically keen to make their mark, just as Pele has done.

So now that I've told you in some detail what I saw and learned, in my travels to Brazil, you'll not be surprised when I say that I shall never forget the country which, remember, has won the World Cup three times.

I won't forget my travels in Italy, too, with Stoke City, for when we went there for last year's Anglo-Italian tournament, we ran into a spot of trouble, when we were playing Roma. There was almost a riot – or so it seemed, at the time, for the Italians are very highly-strung people, and some of them were not exactly in an hospitable mood.

I could never quite fathom out what got them going

– unless it was that they took exception to some of the refereeing decisions. I do know that plate-glass windows were shattered, that the police went into action and used tear gas, as fans fought, and that we had to stay in Roma's ground until the police had cleared all the trouble-makers out. I believe Roma were fined, after that spot of bother . . . and that one of the fans finished up by receiving a two-year gaol sentence.

I think the best crowds I've known, outside Britain, are the fans in Switzerland and Sweden. They're sporting folk, and they can appreciate good play from the opposition, as well as from their own players.

You may remember the German supporters at Wembley, during the 1966 World Cup Final against England. They certainly made themselves heard, especially when West Germany fought back to equalize and take us to extra-time. Probably you remember the noise those fans made with what I can only describe as cowhorns. Well, if you thought they made a row at Wembley, you should just hear them

All eyes on Geoff Hurst (West Ham) as he gets ready to cause trouble for the Stoke City defence

Arsenal's John Radford watches as Gordon Banks punches clear

on their home territory! The racket the German supporters make when their own team has got possession of the ball, and is making for the opposition's goal, is little short of fantastic, believe me.

I sometimes think that part of the idea is to make the visiting defenders panic a little, in the hope that the home side will plonk the ball in the net. The Germans are as fervent as you can find, when it comes to giving their team support.

One of the things you have to get used to, as a visiting English footballer, is the sight and sound of firecrackers on many grounds on the Continent and in South America. You cannot afford to be put off by the crescendo of noise which the fans make, as they let off those firecrackers.

Despite the hazards of travelling abroad to play football – and there are hazards, at times – I can honestly say that I wouldn't have missed a moment of it all. Jet travel, first-class hotels, big games, big crowds . . . it all adds up to a tremendous experience. You see places which other people only dream about and I'm grateful for the privilege of having been able to sample so much of the world, while being paid for doing it!

'Have you heard this one?' Denis Law listens to George Best as Ken Aston and Pat Crerand take things easy

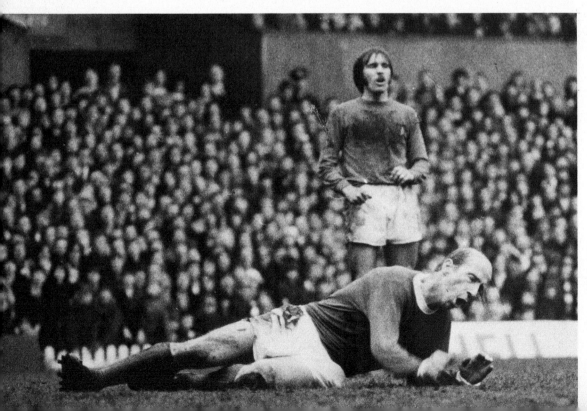

'The joke's on me!' Bobby Charlton hits the deck

They shall not pass! Gary Sprake in determined mood in the Leeds goal

Nothing But The Best

by FRANCIS LEE

In the summer of 1971 a new player pitched up at Maine Road. He was a former colleague of mine in our days with Bolton Wanderers, had been the subject of much transfer speculation in the weeks immediately prior to joining us and was, of course, Wyn Davies.

Much was naturally made of his arrival, and I think it would be fair to say that we Manchester City players were not slow in coming forward to express our opinions when asked. I know that I went on record as reporting my pleasure at Wyn's arrival.

So far as I was concerned there was more to it than a renewal of old friendships, there was the question of his presence adding more weight, in more than one sense, to the Maine Road attack. All of which brings me to an interesting point.

Over the years immediately preceding Wyn's arrival, Manchester City had been quite a successful club. Indeed when one considers the trophies that they had picked up it would be closer the truth to term them an extremely successful outfit. Perhaps a little remembrance would not be out of place.

We will 'forget' their League Championship of

the 1936–7 season, their FA Cup wins of 1904, 1934, even 1956. We will concentrate on what has happened around Maine Road since say 1966, and, if you bear with me, you will see where the signing of Wyn Davies comes into all this.

In that glorious soccer year of 1966 City won the League Division Two title, and started a veritable run of pot collecting. After a season of consolidation, they took the League Championship in 1968, the FA Cup in 1969 and both the League Cup and the European Cup Winners' Cup in 1970. The summer of 1971 was a barren year, no trophies to be harvested.

It was soon after the end of this 'barren' season that we bought Wyn. And here's the point. It proved that Joe Mercer and Malcolm Allison were still in there fighting and improving.

They could, having had a long look back at their successes over the recent few seasons, have said they had done well and what if the 1970–1 season had not been as successful, they surely must come good again.

Had they wished to have said this they would have been supported by the knowledge that many adverse

Francis Lee in training at Maine Road

Table tennis is one of the games George Best enjoys as a way of keeping fit

George Best finds the West Ham defence blocks his way to goal

factors had gone against the skill of the club and its staff during that season. Perhaps the most vital was the alarming amount of injuries we at Maine Road had sustained. It was enough to knock many a club off its feet and it did no good to us.

As I say, they could have used all these explanations for maintaining a *status quo*. They could but they did not. And for one important reason – that Manchester City is one of the greatest clubs in this country and it must be kept at that peak.

This not only means exploiting the talent you have but also preparing for the day when you will need refurnishment in several, or just one, departments. This can be and is done in two ways, either by the recruitment and the advancement of your own juniors and/or by the purchase of what we might term ready-made players of great skill and ability.

One has only to appreciate the excellent manner in which players such as Willie Donachie, Derek Jeffries and Ian Mellor came through last season to see how well this first part, the cultivation of local boys, has been working. Indeed it is interesting to look down the list of City's playing staff to see how well this policy of breeding one's own players has worked.

At the time of writing both the City goalkeepers, Joe Corrigan and Ronnie Healey were local lads; at defensive stations we had Dave Connor, Glyn Pardoe, David Gibbons, Tommy Booth, Colin Barrett, Stuart Curtin, Mike Doyle, Willie Donachie, Derek Jeffries and Alan Oakes all having come up through the juniors, while in attack the list seemed to go on *ad infinitum*.

It is shorter to record who was not, among the front line, the product of the Maine Road nursery. In addition to myself there was Colin Bell, Freddie Hill and Mike Summerbee.

Which, as the man said, leads me quietly to my second point. Having trained and nursed through the lads from their own juniors, City realized that some attacking positions still needed to be filled, and that the quickest way of doing so was to buy. Which they did.

Colin Bell came from Bury, and we all know what a truly magnificent buy he has proved to be. A veritable engine-room on his own, he has the greatest stamina of

Wyn Davies in characteristic action for Manchester City against Leeds United

A jubilant Joe Mercer acknowledges cheers from the crowd as the Manchester City team parades through the streets with the European Cup Winners' Cup in 1970

Bobby Moore, West Ham and England skipper, in thoughtful mood

'I'll huff and I'll puff and I'll blow the ball in' Bobby Charlton seems to be saying to himself

Manchester City's Tony Book and Terry Cooper of Leeds United

any player on the City books, indeed I would suggest of almost any player anywhere. And he can play quite a bit can't he!

Mike Summerbee, whose father was a professional with Preston North End, was one of the first Mercer-Allison buys. He came from Swindon Town and like Colin soon settled down to bring happiness not only to the club but to its thousands of supporters. He has ranged along the forward line at various times, has taken innumerable knocks, can lay off a ball with the best, draw a defence with the same ease, and it's nice to know he is in the side.

Freddie Hill came from Halifax but is perhaps better known for his brilliant days at Bolton Wanderers where we also, like Wyn and myself, were team-mates together. Fred has said himself that when he went to Halifax he felt he had left the big time clubs behind for good, but then he was brought back to Maine Road

and has done a great job not only in his first-team appearances but in passing on his expertise to the youngsters coming up in the reserves.

Yet, with all these home-grown players and those purchased, defenders like George Heslop, Tony Book, and Arthur Mann as well as the others I have mentioned or perhaps unintentionally have not – we still felt, at times, that we were lacking something up front.

That, as well as the injuries, some might say as much as the injuries, did nothing to help us pick up any pots during that 1970–1 season – and Joe and Malcolm were alive to it. They went out into the market and bought Wyn Davies.

As I said earlier, this proved my point that a soccer club must never rest on its past glories, and that in so far as Manchester City are concerned, there is no question of that. What has been achieved in the past can be surpassed in the future. And that's the way it must be for City.

Certainly the club has a magnificent past. I suppose it will surprise some of my younger readers when I tell them that before the war, the Second World War that is, they were much more widely known than Manchester United. At least, say I as a youngish man, that's what I have been told.

Looking at the records seems to support this statement. Although both were formed about 1880 – City under the name of Ardwick and United as Newton Heath, United was the first to win the First Division Championship, in 1908 and as last season drew to a close held a 7–2 Championship winning lead over City.

Yet the bulk of these came after the war, in the early days of the then Matt Busby's reign as manager. They won it for the second time in 1911, and the others came in 1952, 1956, 1957, 1965, 1967, as Sir Matt then approached the close of his managerial career.

City, on the other hand, won their first League title in 1937 and their second in 1968; they won the FA Cup in 1934 – when goalkeeper Frank Swift fainted at the end of the game with sheer excitement – but, and this is the point, from 1930 until 1939 they were regular members of the First Division while United were in the Second Division for six of these seasons.

Obviously I am not trying to score any City versus United points. I may be a City player but I was born on the United side of Manchester and have a great respect for them. I use the above just to show how times can change and that, as some of my younger readers may be inclined to think, City are by no means a come-lately club.

Funny, but when I look back to the time I walked out at Bolton, asserting that I would rather quit the game than re-sign, I cannot help but wonder at the way the coin drops.

At that time I felt I had served Wanderers well and that I deserved the reward of being allowed to move to

Francis Lee heads for goal

Cup ties or neckties – both are colourful events in the life of George Best

This is my life! George Best on the ball for Northern Ireland

a bigger club. I was ambitious, and I was determined, believing that right was on my side. Well, in the end I got my move, and it turned out to be not that far away, to Manchester City.

Some of my ambitions have been realized with City. I have won almost every honour in the game, from a Cup Final medal to an international cap. And as I have won them, so City has as well. I would like to think that we have been good for one another.

Yet, as we started last season who was it that City went out and bought to help us, they hoped, to greater glory still. None other than my old Bolton colleague Wyn Davies, and with Colin Bell from near-by Bury on the other side of that inside trio it really is a small world isn't it. And it's one that City, like all other clubs worth their salt, wish to stand astride.

Their desire is genuine, and worthy of applause. It's nothing but the best.

LAWS OF PLAY 1

If the ball goes directly into goal from a corner-kick would a goal be allowed?

(See page 106 for answer)

Farewell Sir Matt

— and Thanks

by GEORGE BEST

The day Sir Matt Busby handed us Manchester United players over to his successor, Frank O'Farrell will, as they say, live long in my memory. Looking back to that day in July, 1971, I still feel what I thought then. That there was something almost symbolic, certainly typically Sir Matt, in the gesture.

We were all gathered together at The Cliff, our training headquarters. Sir Matt, accompanied by his life-long right-hand man, Jimmy Murphy, made the necessary introductions, said all that was required and then not only walked away but left almost immediately on holiday.

This meant, of course, that our new boss, Mr O'Farrell, had us to himself from then on; he was not only in charge as we all knew, but Sir Matt had effectively displayed to the world and his wife that this was so.

You may remember that this was at the time when the Football Association had just closed the Old Trafford ground for a couple of weeks and the question of alternative grounds had to be considered and arranged.

Had Sir Matt wished to prolong his immediate association as the man in charge there would have been ample excuse for him to have done so. He did not. Having handed over control after all those magnificent years he was apparently determined to do so in such a manner as to leave no doubt as to Frank O'Farrell's total assumption of full authority.

One has to admire him. There had been a great deal of talk about the difficulties any new manager might feel with Sir Matt towering above, albeit unintentionally, as General Manager. But with the wisdom we at Old Trafford have always associated with him, Sir Matt soon put an end to any such talk by quitting the General Managership of the club at the same time as he handed over team affairs to Mr O'Farrell.

Sir Matt's career is almost too well known to require reiteration, but there are, I suppose, those among us, and those outside, who do not realize just what he has meant to so many people fortunate enough to come into contact with him.

Take my case for instance. It has been said that natural talent will out, and it has been said that I have

Alan Ball attempts a cross when playing for England against Scotland

Right: Balance and control are all-important in a match. George Best on the ball during practice

Sir Matt Busby proudly showing Mr and Mrs Frank O'Farrell round Old Trafford in June, 1971

Sir Matt with 'local' rival Joe Mercer

natural talent as a footballer. If the two statements are correct then I suppose I would be playing football now for some senior club even if Sir Matt had not shown interest in me, but one must wonder whether one's career would have taken the particular turns that it has.

Take that Manchester to Belfast telephone call for instance. You must know the one I mean. It was made by Sir Matt the day after I'd raced back home to Belfast after a mere twenty-four hours at Old Trafford. I'd gone across with Alex McMordie, a couple of kids in search of soccer stardom, but soon we found that being away from our native Ireland was too big a price to pay. So we did the thing natural for us. We hopped it back home again, pretty smartly too if I remember.

Thank goodness Sir Matt was not to be 'beaten' that easily. He was soon on the 'phone to my father and made enough sense for me to return to Manchester, and eventual soccer stardom. Of course it is easy for one to say now, when I've made a bit of a name for myself, that of course Sir Matt would have chased me up to get me back to Manchester. But one should remember that I was a mere slip of a lad then, a prospect who might make it, or might not. No more than that.

One suspects that at some clubs, perhaps at a large number, the attitude might have been to have left someone in a less noble berth than Sir Matt to have gone to the trouble of chasing up an errant kid. But that was not the way the Boss worked. I have not known him all his footballing career of course, but I doubt if he was ever any different in his approach to the game and to people.

Certainly I have always found him a completely honest person. Indeed I suppose I would rate that his finest quality. A lot has been said about his knowledge of football and of people, of his diplomatic qualities, of his business acumen. All true, but if I had to pick the one quality about him which I admired above all else I think it would be his honest approach to a problem or a person.

As some of you may recall that I was not immune to the occasional call into the Boss's office when I was a bit younger than I am now. I really don't think there was ever anything serious, but like all youngsters there were times when I was adjudged to be in need of a session with Sir Matt.

As I have said before, he could be a strict person on such occasions, he certainly didn't invite you in to hand out the sweeties, but if the visit was the result of a report to him about you there was always one format. He would tell you of the nature of the complaint and then invite your opinion upon it or version of events. And when you'd had your say he would invariably take your word for what had happened, or had not, working on the assumption that he would be honest with you and therefore assumed that you would offer him the courtesy of being truthful with him.

Mind you, he could come down like the proverbial ton of bricks on anyone who let him or his beloved Manchester United down, but who could complain about that? One knew the score and one accepted it . . . honest does as honest did.

Well, what do you say about the man which could possibly be new? Surely it must be impossible. If ever a man built a football club into a world-wide institution it was he, if ever a man rose from humble surrounds to walk with kings, and not to lose the common touch it was Sir Matt.

He was born in Orbiston, Lanarkshire, in a pitman's cottage in that small Scottish village, and but for a delayed visa he might well have gone to America instead of moving to Manchester – as a player with our big local rivals, Manchester City!

I suppose he could have been excused for feeling, upon signing for the Maine Road club, that he was well on his way to fame and fortune, for even in those days, 1928, footballers weren't exactly unknown members of society, even if they were nowhere near as highly paid. But it was not all roses by any means.

If I remember what I heard correctly, Sir Matt was in fact struggling a bit to make his playing mark with City, until a switch of position caused the horizons to brighten and the big time to move nearer to the man who was to prove more than equal to any occasion.

He made his first team début for City in 1930, played his first international for Scotland – he received thirteen caps in all – in 1933, and in 1936 was transferred to Liverpool where he almost became a senior official after the Second World War. Indeed he was about to take up his duties there when the post of manager of Manchester United was offered to him and Liverpool sportingly agreed to his taking the post.

His record since then has been quite fantastic. To recall just a few of the highlights. There was Manchester United beating Blackpool to win the FA Cup in 1948,

41

the same year in which he was offered and accepted the post of manager of the Great Britain Olympic Games team which reached the semi-final of that competition. The powers that be had already recognized the man among them.

There followed a couple of League Championship wins – in 1956 and 1957 – at a time when arguments raged as to whether the then United side was better than that which Sir Matt had run in the late 1940s and early 1950s. Then came the tragedy of the Munich Air Disaster of 1958 when Sir Matt himself fought a brave and finally successful fight against death, but was left scarred by the passing on that Munich runway of so many friends – players, pressmen and others.

One who died that day was the already almost immortal Frank Swift, 'Big Swifty', the giant of a Manchester City goalkeeper who had retired and turned to sportswriting. It was Sir Matt who as a City player at Wembley displayed a magnificent, typically human gesture, when he turned and played a ball back to the then teenaged and nervous Frank Swift in the City goal to give the lad an early touch of the ball.

Aided by Jimmy Murphy, Sir Matt set about rebuilding a new United out of the ashes and although it would perhaps be presumptuous for me to say too much, one cannot help but reflect that as we have, for instance, won the European Cup since then, a bad job was not done.

Now Sir Matt has retired from the managership but I doubt if he's really ever going to be able to forsake an interest in football. It has been too big a part of his life, he is too large a slice of the game's history.

Surely if ever a man deserved the accolade of the knighthood that was bestowed upon him it was Sir Matt; surely if ever a man deserved the approbation he received from all over the world it was he. Surely, of no man can it better be said 'Well done Sir Matt'.

LAWS OF PLAY 2

If the ball swerves over the goal-line but back into play, should the game continue?

(See page 106 for answer)

George Best photographed outside 'Edwardia' – one of his Manchester boutiques

Bob McNab (Arsenal) in the thick of things – supported by John Radford – in a league match against Chelsea at Highbury

★★

The Highbury Atmosphere

by BOB Mc NAB

★★

Talk to most people about atmosphere in soccer and they immediately think that it concerns the build-up to a big match and the tensions which send all those elusive butterflies fluttering in players' tummies.

In a way, they're correct. That's atmosphere all right. But there is another vitally important atmosphere that is taken too much for granted – the one within the club. If that isn't there, the one that affects the supporters may never arrive.

Well, we are lucky at Arsenal. We have atmosphere in the club *and* among our fans. It's great, really . . . so let's take the one inside the club first.

There is a tremendous air of friendliness at Highbury. It is rather difficult to describe, but it's there; a feeling that everyone – and I mean everyone – is part of the club. You sense that the lowest paid member of the stadium staff is just as much part of the club as the highest paid star. This, of course, is the way it should be. Football is a team game and running a great club such as Arsenal needs a team effort on and off the field. There is this sort of impression that everyone is part of one big, happy family. For example, there is the lady who washes the kit. She always gives

us a pleasant 'Good morning' and the players have a chat with her.

It all breeds an enlightened kind of discipline. I don't think any player would dare take a liberty with the club because of this approach. They are fully aware that although no one may be wielding a big stick, the authority is there all the time. Call it a form of trust, if you like, but it works and brings out a wonderful club spirit. Of course, there is the usual tension at our matches. This varies according to the importance of the action, yet I can honestly say that nowhere will anyone find supporters to beat our six-bob fans.

Those behind our goals are magnificent, especially our North Bank lads. They just cannot be bettered by any lot of supporters including those wonderful followers who have built such a fine reputation for themselves on The Kop at Liverpool.

I am not so sure that the supporters in the seats at Highbury come up to the standard set by our goal-end fans. Those people in the seats take a lot of pleasing at times. From my own experience, I can say that I have watched other London clubs play pretty poor stuff

45

Congratulations and jubilations! George Graham celebrates with Bob McNab after scoring for Arsenal against Leeds United

before their own supporters and they have been clapped off the field. That is the way to support a club! I have often come away from one of those matches thinking that if we had turned in such a performance at Highbury we would have taken a bit of stick.

What I believe it boils down to is that those Arsenal fans who expect five-star shows all the time have been spoiled by success. They get frustrated with failure and some of them are inclined to take it out on the players. Not so, the supporters behind our goals. They are with us always and I cannot emphasize too much how much the players appreciate their loyalty.

For the atmosphere that remains in my mind regarding a match, I must go away from Highbury . . . to Brussels. We were playing Anderlecht in the first leg of the Fairs Cup Final. The date was April 22nd, 1970, and it is ringed in my book of memories as the day I will never forget. The ground is a small compact one and it was absolutely packed, bulging at the seams with 30,000. I have never felt such an intense atmosphere in any game before or since. It just hit you as you walked out on to the pitch.

I have played in two Wembley finals, but they didn't compare with this match in Anderlecht. This *was* atmosphere. Don't ask me why. It could be that we were playing on foreign soil, I don't know. What I do know is that I have never experienced anything quite like it.

Arsenal's Bob Wilson at his Enfield home with his family. He is here seen autographing copies of his autobiography

Arsenal's Eddie Kelly putting on the style as he takes aim for the Barnsley goal in a League Cup match

We lost 3–1. Everything turned out fine, however, as we won the second-leg 3–0 and took the cup on aggregate. The atmosphere at the end of the second-leg was also fantastic. I remember when the whistle went for full time I just sprinted like mad for the tunnel to get clear of our fans.

Yet the sprint I did that night was almost tortoise-slow compared to the dash I made for the dressing-room when we beat Tottenham at White Hart Lane to clinch the First Division Championship just five days before our FA Cup Final.

The build-up to this match was tremendous, just out of this world. It takes some believing, but we arrived at Spurs ground at 6.15. I remember checking the time as we pulled up only 150 yards from the ground. By the time we had struggled through the crowds to the sanctuary – and it was sanctuary – of our dressing-room it was 6.55.

It had taken us 40 minutes to walk 150 yards!

This kind of situation worries me, as I am always expecting someone to get hurt. Indeed, I am surprised that no one ever does when crowds jam up like they did that night.

As for the match – I was playing left-back and that suited me because it meant that I was near the tunnel as time ran out. With about a minute to go, I was half-watching play and half-watching the tunnel. And when the whistle did go, boy did Bob McNab turn on the tap as he raced for cover! Our players at the other side of the pitch were not so lucky. The fans almost 'murdered' them and it was twenty minutes before they got into the dressing-room. Just in bits, they were.

Still, it's nice to be successful. Winning trophies is the end product of football and be sure that the Arsenal players will be trying all they know to bring some more honours to Highbury . . . for the club and for their fans.

This will mean more tension-packed matches and more excitement on the terraces. My only hope is that even if I am left-back in them I will be on the 'right' side of the pitch when the final whistle goes – close as a whisker to that tunnel escape route!

It's Conga time at Highbury as the Arsenal and Ipswich players combine for the final dance round the Ipswich goalmouth

People ask what it's like

to play alongside

George ☆ Best

by DEREK DOUGAN

I've often referred to him as the 'white Pele'. Now that Pele has 'abdicated' there's no need to make this comparison. Georgie Best is . . . well, Georgie Best. And when you've said that you have said everything the name conjures up in the minds of people throughout the world.

Television has given him an international reputation and when he plays abroad thousands of people come to see him confirm the impression they have of him, as a ball-playing genius. They expect him to work magic with the ball. He does not often disappoint them.

Time and again I'm asked: 'What's it like playing alongside him?' and 'What's he like?'

The two questions go together. When I've answered the first, I've answered the second.

It's like playing with a maestro. In the Northern Ireland side he rips through defences, manoeuvres his way into positions that cause havoc in any defence and enables me to capitalize on the space he creates. I know that at least two or three opposing defenders are having to concentrate on him, worrying about what he will do next – and that's his elusive strength, the other side is never sure what he's going to do.

I've heard cynics complain that George is a selfish player, that he likes to hang on to the ball and go it alone. Obviously they have not watched him closely – and take their standards from players who believe in getting rid of the ball the moment they receive it.

George is too intelligent a player to do it this way. A 'selfish' player is one who immediately passes the ball to a colleague who is well and truly marked, unable to do ànything with the ball except lose it. Instead of using his own intelligence, he gets rid of the ball to let another player do the work for him.

George has periphery vision – that is, he 'reads' a game spontaneously, judges situations from all angles at any given moment. He knows when to hang on to the ball and weave his way through and when to make the best use of it with a pass.

He works for his fellow players, drawing a defence before putting through a 'killer' pass or making space for an attack. He won't let the ball go simply because he's under pressure and leave another player to take

49

*George Best puts the ball in the back of the net in an Ireland v. England international,
but the goal was disallowed for an infringement*

George Best on the ball for Manchester United against Wolves

George Best ready for action for Ireland

the blame for botching a move. If he were selfish he would simply be standing around waiting for passes. I think that dispenses with a foolish argument.

I first met George at the Norbreck hotel in Blackpool seven years ago, when I was with Peterborough United on a special training course, and he was there with Manchester United.

If I remember correctly, the first thing he said to me was that he could not understand why I wasn't in the Irish squad. This was the time I had been dropped from the Northern Ireland team, for reasons which it would be irrelevant to go into here.

In October, 1965, I was with him in the Irish side, beating Scotland three-two. First impressions, they say, are best. My first impression of George as a player was a good one. He impressed me from the start – and remember, this was before he became a celebrity.

Much has happened to him since then, though basically he is unchanged. He enjoys fame and riches, has a house which is always given a price tag when mentioned in the Press; receives a fan mail which makes any other player's mail seem like a small trickle. But when I'm with him I can detect the pressure under which he lives. In the Irish squad he's treated as he likes to be treated, not as a celebrity but as an equal, another member of the team which provides for him a kind of refuge. He can muck in, horse

around, feel for a while his Irish background, make contact with his roots.

George is the kind of player that football must occasionally produce – if only to prove that in the last analysis men are better than machines.

In recent years football has become faster, more demanding and I think, more exciting than in the past. The competition is certainly greater now than at any time in the game's history. But with so much concentration on defence and formations, the game is in danger of becoming 'mechanised'.

Players are sometimes forced to fit into patterns with little or no room for individual prowess. The great sides are those which ally formative control with individual flair. This explains Manchester United's success. George is a team player and also an individualist. Two years ago Paddy Crerand disagreed with me that George was the 'white Pele'. At the time he didn't put him in that bracket. Now he agrees that George is 'out of this world'.

He has the sort of individuality which helps to revitalise the game. He's as near as we are likely to get to the complete footballer. He's better with his left foot than Pele. This is not a fellow countryman's eulogy, more of an objective assessment of George's skill and what it means to the game. Abroad, he represents the best in British soccer. For foreign tours, he has the right initials.

LAWS OF PLAY 3

May the defending players stand less than 10 yards from the ball at any time?

(See page 106 for answer)

Fair Play
For The Players

by DENIS LAW

In the summer of 1970, as the World Cup was being fought for in far-off Mexico, I was entering a football battle of my own, but much nearer home, at The Cliff and at a friend's gymnasium in near-by Stockport. I was battling for full physical fitness once more and intended if necessary to continue the fight right through the summer months, right up to the start of the following football season.

The background behind this particular personal battle may well be familiar to many of you. For the previous two seasons I had not been able to do full justice either to myself or to the Manchester United club because of niggling injuries which had bedevilled my match days and my training spells during that time.

I do not intend to bore you with the details, suffice it to say that the set-backs were such as to lead a lot of people to think they had seen the best of Denis Law. One person who certainly did not agree with this assumption was myself. If only, I felt, I could get myself fully fit again then we could indeed show the cynics how wrong they were.

So we arrived at that fateful summer of 1970.

Because of England's World Cup commitments the Football League programme ended earlier than usual that spring, something which suited me admirably. It meant that we would have a break lasting up to four months. Earlier I had fully intended to sacrifice my summer holiday in my attempt to regain full fitness, but had felt rather guilty in that this could mean at best my family going on holiday on their own, but with this extra long summer break it enabled me to go away with them for a couple of weeks and then come back to work.

Believe me, work I did. While the rest of the English League players – those not in Mexico that is – were enjoying their well-deserved holidays I was sweating out a lonely six-day-a-week training stint. On Mondays, Tuesdays and Wednesdays I was hard at it at The Cliff, on Thursdays, Fridays and Saturdays having the weight training sessions in that Stockport gymnasium. A lot of people said to me that I must be dedicated to be undertaking such a system in my 'time off months'. Incidentally, I was a little peeved that anyone got to know about it in the first place as I had tried to keep the whole thing secret. But I was dedicated – of course I was – and still am. As is every professional worth his salt.

As I said to these folk, professional footballers these days, particularly these days of high financial rewards, are in the main very responsible people, players well aware of their responsibilities. Oh yes, we do certainly have responsibilities. I would place them, roughly, into five categories. There is the player's responsibility to himself, to his club, to his family, to his team and to his fans.

Let us take them one by one, not necessarily in any particular order, but as I have mentioned them just now. And first then is the player's responsibility to himself. This is a fairly simple one, for it is a question of keeping himself in the peak of physical fitness at all possible times, to maintain an equilibrium in his code of living, and in his conduct at the club and with the players and staff. That is why I spent those summer months working so hard and, as they said 'in my own time'. I was determined to kill once and for all that then present injury bogey and start the fresh season fully fit.

For this reason, any of my friends wishing to come round and see me or give me a ring on the 'phone know that they will find me in on any of six evenings of the week. The exception is Saturday when, after a match, if we have been playing at Old Trafford or somewhere nearish to Manchester, you will find me

out with my wife for the evening. For the rest of the week it is home of an evening, and, indeed, not all that late to bed. Perhaps a good book or an interesting television programme may keep me downstairs a little later than usual but normally we are 'early birds'.

The player's responsibility to his club? In many ways that is similar to the responsibility to himself, but perhaps with additions. Basically, of course, is the need to maintain himself at full mental and physical fitness but in addition – and we are assuming the skills being there – he must fit in with his team-mates, both on and off the field.

Much was made of the skills of several of the boys at Old Trafford over the years, but one should never be drawn into making the mistake of assuming that because there was so much skill there there was no need for blend. Any such assumption would be complete nonsense. Sir Matt Busby was never one to permit a situation to arise in which stars shone for themselves alone or by themselves alone. Of course he would not wish to limit the individual abilities of the George Bests, the Bobby Charltons and the like, but both he and they, all of us in fact, aimed to make it a team effort. The same goes today.

This is what a star player must do, however great his ability or however great he thinks his ability to be, and they are not necessarily the same thing. A star footballer must be able to use his skills but also to use them

LAWS OF PLAY 4

If the ball is about to enter the goal but is deflected by a dog (or spectator) can the Referee award a goal?

(See page 106 for answer)

'I've made my point by scoring' Denis Law might be saying following his second goal against Crystal Palace

within the framework of the side. Which brings me rather neatly to the player's responsibilities to the fans.

Of course, the football fans love to see individual brilliance, indeed that is often one of the most exciting features of his afternoon's entertainment. But it is not the premier attraction, not at least for the vast majority of supporters. To them the prime enjoyment is received and registered by seeing their team win.

that week-end, there can be tensions as the players mentally build up for the match. Nothing argumentative or anything like that but tensions in the mind, etc.

In addition there are the times players are away on tours, international duties and the like. And, of course, there is all the trouble and often temporary heartbreak of leaving one city and moving to another when a transfer is involved. In addition, there is the question

'Oh! Mr Woo . . .' Manchester United players seem to have been in a mudlark and the laundryman is in for a busy time

The star must never forget this. However great he is, however brilliant a show he can personally turn on it counts, in the final analysis for very little if it has not been employed to obtain a result for his side.

Last but by no means least one comes to one's family, and what long-suffering people players' wives have to be at times. Certainly there is a lot on the credit side but there are also some debit items. And the same goes for the children as well.

Every other week-end, their husbands or fathers are away from Friday lunch-time, probably earlier, until late Saturday evening, possibly early Sunday morning. And, in many cases, even if father's side are at home

of uprooting the children's education, often at a vital time.

I often think that it is the wives who have the worst of it, though I suppose that we have our problems, if one can call them that, in our responsibilities. Personally I do not. I believe that players should not only have such responsibilities but indeed be very willing to accept them.

We know that we have gained a lot from the game and, if we have any sense of the order of things, expect to put something back in. And providing there are more of us thinking this way than the other then both the game and ourselves will benefit.

Denis Law challenges a Wolves player for the ball

Trevor Francis (Birmingham) *closely marked by a Queens Park Rangers defender*

The Way Ahead

by TREVOR FRANCIS

Have you ever been called 'The Wonder Boy', 'The Whiz-bang Kid' or the 'Teenage Goal King'? I have, and it's nowhere near as pleasant as it may at first sound. Indeed, when last season all these phrases seemed to have disappeared, in so far as I was concerned anyway, I was really glad.

They started, of course, soon after I made my début in the Birmingham City first team, and managed to slot in a few goals. That was in the season of 1970–71 and I finished up with a tally of something like fifteen goals from fifteen Second Division games. Of course that was good going. A goal a game average must be, and I'd be telling lies if I didn't admit it was so. But it certainly brought the pressures.

I like to think I am pretty level-headed, and indeed one or two sports journalists who have done features on me have said I seem to be. I hope so – for I always aim to keep my feet on the ground, and it was certainly needed in those early months of my appearance in the Second Division.

As an apprentice at the club, at any football club in fact, you are normally able to go out and about your business and your pleasure away from the ground without exciting any attention. But once you get into the first team things become different, and if you have the good fortune, as I did, to get immediately among the goal-getters then everywhere you go you are a target for stares and for comment.

You even get the odd – and perhaps that really is the correct word – individual who wishes to start an argument with you whenever you appear in a public place. I remember a sportswriter once telling me that George Best, whom he knew fairly well, said that he experienced the same trouble. I haven't yet really figured out just what such people are trying to prove, but it seems certain that they are certainly trying to make some peculiar point. Then, as I said at the start of this article, come the name-droppers.

Normally this phrase means people who are always boasting about the important people they know, but in this instance I'm referring to those types who, having read a phrase or a headline in a paper or a sports magazine and then seeing you out, shout across 'Hi, Wonder Boy', 'Whiz-kid' or something equally stupid. One should, of course, take no notice of them, particularly as so many of them mean it as a compliment –

59

though there are the others – but it does begin to grate a bit after a while. You feel that if anyone's going to talk to you it would be much better and a lot more pleasant if they would confine themselves to your ordinary, and proper, name.

As I have said, although I had plenty of this when

at basketball but hates football, so it doesn't run right through the family does it, though my father gave me tons of encouragement. I really do owe a great deal to him. As soon as I could walk almost he had me out with a ball, practising the game, and some evenings later on he would insist we worked only with one foot

An all-action shot of Steve Heighway of Liverpool in a league match against Leeds United

I first popped on to the senior soccer scene it did disappear quite a bit last season, for which I am eternally grateful. But, naturally, I'm even more grateful for the fact that I came into the position in which people did recognize me, and wanted to speak with me. How did it all begin? There, as the man says, lies a story.

I was born in the West Country, in Plymouth in fact, and my Dad was a professional footballer as well, a defensive wing-half with Argyle. I have incidentally a fifteen-year-old brother Ian who is good

for that session and with the other for the next session. It is a policy I would pass on to any young lad who is not a natural two-footer, and how many of them are there in the game? In the old days, I'm told, it was not unusual to see a player, even a recognized class player practising with a boot on one foot and the thinnest of slippers on the other. The idea was to encourage the use of the foot wearing the boot, which was, you may be sure, his normally 'weak' foot or peg.

To get back to my story. At the truly early age of

61

Iam McFaul (Newcastle United)

seven to eight I was in my school – the Pennycross Primary – side, and I don't think that after that I was ever really out of a school side until signing for Birmingham. I know I was picked, again at a very early age, relatively speaking, for the local Public Secondary School to which I graduated and by the time I was

game, I understand, was Don Dorman, the chief scout of Birmingham City, and he was there again when we played Birmingham schools in the English Schools Trophy competition and beat them 5–0 I think it was. I was invited to have a trial with Birmingham, duly went up there, met the then manager, Mr Stan Cullis,

'Excuse me old chap, let me see what's going on!' Mick Mills (Ipswich) keeps a watchful eye on West Ham attackers Billy Bonds and Clyde Best

fifteen I was playing mid-field in the Plymouth schools senior side and I went on to captain the Devon county side.

It was around this time, and it's only a few seasons back really, that I went to St. Albans to take part in the England Schools Trials. And, you could say, it all began to happen again from that time. Watching this

had my trial, and must have made a favourable sort of impression because I soon joined their staff as an apprentice professional.

Then, with almost breath-taking speed, came my rise into Second Division football. As far as I can remember the sequence of events it went along the lines of my having a game in the Birmingham third team, this being followed by a couple in the reserve side, then next week I was substitute for the first team at Cardiff and the next week I was in the first team. So in something like five games in less than a month I had gone from third team to first team, and Second Division, football.

The rest most of you may well know. I was drafted in and out of the first team, the feeling being that I was still rather young and it was best, the club thought, to blood me in easy stages. Yet the funny thing was that I found it more difficult to play in the reserves when I went back into their side than I did playing in the first team on each occasion upon which I stepped up. I think there is a quite simple explanation for this, the fact that you have better and probably more experienced players around you in the senior side at any club, more people to assist in taking the weight off you if that is necessary. Mind you, I think that having the senior players around you can perhaps have an inhibiting effect as well.

I certainly found that I was inclined to play a lot of 'get it, give it' football in my early days in the first team. You would receive the ball from a colleague but you pushed it away to another as quickly as you could too often. This is understandable really. You are young, new and inexperienced in the ways of the larger football world; you are still feeling your way around, and don't wish to gum up the team works by doing the wrong thing.

I recall another sportswriter once telling me that Manchester United's fine striker and all-round player Brian Kidd experienced this sort of feeling in his first few games. But he soon got rid of it and so have I now. What a great job Brian has done for his club.

Last season, indeed towards the end of the season before that, it was different as I settled in and the goals were coming along fairly regularly, though one must not forget, indeed one should always be reminded that there is more to any football team than the person or persons who actually pop the ball into the net.

That's most certainly how I feel, and perhaps I could give you an explanation, and an illustration all in one. At the start of last season I was not getting among the goals with the same frequency as I had the season before, but I was not unduly concerned. The reason was simple. I knew in my heart that I was playing well, even though the goals were not coming. Now had I not have been playing well, and the goals not coming because of that, then I truly would have been worried. Don't get me wrong – of course I like scoring goals and wish to, but so long as the team are scoring them and providing I am contributing a full part then I am not perturbed about any lack of personal kudos. Even so, over the long term, I hope to be scoring goals for a long time to come. And, of course, as each season goes by so the opportunity for fans to call me a 'Whiz-Kid' or a 'Wonder Boy' disappears.

If I do well for my club the only other thing I'd like to be called is Trevor Francis – international!

LAWS OF PLAY 5

May a player kick the ball before it touches the ground when it is being dropped by the Referee?
(See page 106 for answer)

Mr Frank O'Farrell, manager of Manchester United

Manchester United — My Job

by FRANK O'FARRELL

On a sunny Saturday afternoon last October Manchester United went to the top of Division One by beating Huddersfield Town by three goals to nil. It happened also to be my birthday, a fact upon which the members of the Press seized and announced, in one or two newspapers, in rather large headlines.

'Happy Birthday' said at least one, if I recall the incident correctly. And, one must admit, it certainly was a particularly happy occasion. Indeed, as we had the week before ended Sheffield United's unbeaten run and the week after did the same to Derby County, it could be said that it was quite a memorable month.

Members of the Press, always alive to a story and to a prediction, suggested by the end of the month that perhaps United were already on the way to the League Championship in new manager Frank O'Farrell's first season at Old Trafford. It was extremely kind of them to suggest this, though personally I preferred, as I said at the time, to await the event, so many things being able to intervene between that October and last May.

We all now know what in fact did happen between

then and now, but long before the last few games were being played I knew that the soccer season of 1971–72 had been a memorable one for me.

The summer of 1971 had seen me take over the managerial chair at Old Trafford, not only becoming the man in charge of one of the most famous and respected football clubs in the world, but also the man who had to succeed to a chair that Sir Matt Busby had occupied with immense, world-renowned, distinction for over twenty years.

Words of advice were not slow in coming my way. They were amusing in their range, interesting to listen to – providing one was still, at the end, one's own counsellor – and sometimes quite surprising in the strength of their advocacy.

There were the people who shook their head in bewilderment when they heard I was to take the job; there were even others, before that, who had urged me not to take it. My mental faculties, if I took it, were suspect obviously in the eyes of some, yet my intelligence high in the eyes of others. I had, in short, become all things to many men by the invitation to accept the Old Trafford post. All this was, of course, due in the main to the aspects of the post.

United, at that time, were not exactly on the crest of a high football wave. Certainly they were eighth in the table and had done well, by most clubs' standards,

would immediately have to undertake a complete re-building job, by some people outside Old Trafford of course. I was told that I'd need a long-term contract to see my plans come to fruition, by other people outside Old Trafford.

Willie Morgan (Manchester United) ready to set up an attack against Wolves

in the League Cup, where they had reached the semi-finals before going out to the ebullient and effective Aston Villa.

However, by United's own yardstick this was not a season of mighty success and worse, in some people's eyes, was the thought that the team might be 'over the top'.

Yes, this was actually being said about the time I took over the post of manager. I was told that I

I have never been a person to shirk a challenge, either in my playing days which ended in senior soccer with Preston North End or when I went straight from the First Division with them to take over the manager-ship of Weymouth in the Southern League. Even then there were people who doubted the wisdom of my choice, but a challenge was there to be met. That was nearly seven seasons ago and, as they say, much water has flowed under the bridge since then. This is most

66

apparent when one looks back over those years to my very first club at Weymouth. Two examples might suffice to show what I mean.

Weymouth was, of course, a club in which the players were part-timers, men who came down to for when we trained on the sands – in front of deserted promenades – we used the sea-front illuminations to light up our training sessions.

Compare this with the situation at The Cliff, the magnificent Manchester United training headquarters.

They shall not pass! Alex Stepney (*Manchester United*) *prepares to defend his goal*

train a couple of evenings a week and then meet again for the match on the Saturday. The only time we had anything like a sustained spell together was if we had the fortune to get a Cup run of any consequence. Then it might be possible to get the lads off work to give us a couple of days together. In the dark winter evenings this normal two-nights-a-week training was not helped by the absence of illumination for the seafront sessions, but we overcame this in one aspect at least,

There we have all the players available at the times we want them and in addition have all the latest indoor and outdoor facilities available. Neither darkness, nor rain, snow, ice or anything else can impede our training schedules.

Yes, there is, by the very nature of things, a major gap between the two clubs, but the difference is felt all the way up the ladder I have trod. On the one hand there is the natural sequence of improvements, as there should be, the higher you get up the ladder; on the other, there are the differences brought about by different priorities, etc. at different clubs, though the winning of matches is a common factor, of course, to them all.

Let me say immediately that I do not regret for one moment starting at the bottom of the ladder and working my way up it. I would not be so presumptuous as to suggest that this is the only way it either can or should be done, but in my case I think I have picked up information, attitudes and more understanding all the way along. For instance, if I am talking to a manager of a Fourth Division club I can appreciate how he is placed say with regard to meeting a transfer fee or indeed a long run of injuries with his smaller staff.

Indeed, I can even understand if I receive a letter from him and the typing is not perhaps as copy-book as one which we at Old Trafford might send out. For while today I can dictate a letter to my secretary or one of the several others we have at United, I well remember how in my early days I often had to get down and two-finger type out my own letters.

As many of you will no doubt know by now, I left Weymouth for Torquay – and had the good fortune to take them to promotion from the Fourth to the Third Division before leaving them to go to Leicester City, where I again had the pleasure of taking the club back up into the First Division.

I would like to think that I made a positive contribution at each club I have managed. Someone once said to me that as I had increased the local interest in the clubs I had achieved something. I hope so.

Will, or even would now, the town of Weymouth (3,500 average attendance), Torquay (8,000), Leicester (25,000–26,000) and United (50,000 plus) feel the impact of Frank O'Farrell upon their soccer scene a good one? So far as the first three are concerned I would like to think so. As regards United then only time will tell. This brings me back to last year, and the top of the table situation which arose at Old Trafford. I received a great deal of credit for this, but it really should have been a credit shared. So many fine people were involved.

There were the United directors who appointed me, Sir Matt himself, now of course a director, for the manner in which he publicly placed the charge of the team completely in my hands; the coaching staff headed by my old colleague Malcolm Musgrove, and, of course, the players themselves.

Take George Best for example. People told me he might be temperamental, difficult to handle and all the rest of it. Nothing, as I soon discovered, could be further from the truth. Within a few days, certainly within a week or so of arriving at Old Trafford, I had realized that George was a dedicated professional, a boy who not only loved his football but worked hard at it. He is never late for training, is nearly always the last one off the training field and, indeed, would still be working with a ball when the rest of the lads are in the bath. And, of course, he can play a bit as well!

I have mentioned George, but for him you can read all the lads. I have always believed in giving players responsibility, providing they return it; in setting examples as to what you want and require, both on the field and away from it.

I have always found that – with the occasional exception, of course, such a system of honesty and trust pays off. I have found no reason at Old Trafford to alter my views. And certainly those first few weeks' results had a lot of folk making early in the season predictions that the policy could be seen to be paying off.

As I have said, though it was early days, one thing was clear to me, that the entire football public as much as those of United colour wanted us to do well; that United had over the years become more than a football club, more like a public institution. The influence of United spreads far beyond Britain – indeed, to the Continent and even further afield. They are an international soccer symbol. And I had been given the job of restoring them to this status.

Time, and you, will tell whether I have been successful in the task.

George Best in thoughtful mood

George Best's Soccer Quiz

1. Do you know who was the first non-international player to be transferred for a fee of £100,000 or more? Which club paid the fee?
2. How many clubs have risen from the Fourth Division to play in Division One?
3. Can you remember which was the first English club side to play in the final of one of the three big European competitions?
4. Which clubs play on the following grounds?
   (*a*) Pittodrie Park; (*b*) Leeds Road; (*c*) St. Andrews; (*d*) Rugby Park; (*e*) Brisbane Road; and (*f*) Boundary Park.
5. I spend most of my playing days searching for League points. They don't always come easily. But in one country you actually win a point if you *lose* the match! Do you know which country this is?
6. Only one Football League club has played an FA Cup-tie in England, Scotland, Ireland and Wales. Which one?
7. The following players have all done well for themselves in the First Division. But can you recall which clubs gave each of them their League débuts?
   (*a*) Ron Davies; (*b*) Kevin Hector; (*c*) Derek Dougan; (*d*) Norman Hunter; (*e*) Colin Bell; and (*f*) Rodney Marsh.
8. Arsenal won fame for winning three consecutive League Championships in the 'thirties and, more recently, the FA Cup and League double. They weren't the first club to achieve these distinctions. Can you name the first club to achieve each of those outstanding feats?
9. Cardiff City, in 1927, were the only non-English club to win the FA Cup. But do you know if any non-English side has ever won the Scottish Cup?
10. Pools punters spend hours searching for draws. They aren't easy to forecast. But do you know if any club has ever completed its League programme without drawing a solitary game?
11. Three years ago I had the good fortune to equal the FA Cup competition proper record with six goals against Northampton Town. Only two other players have done this since the war. One is a colleague of mine at Old Trafford. Can you name them both?
12. It's grand being able to play home matches in one of the biggest and finest stadiums in the country. But Old Trafford isn't quite the biggest. Do you know which is the largest in the Football League?
13. The following are early names of now-famous clubs. Can you identify them?
    (*a*) Thames Ironworks; (*b*) Heaton Norris on the Ash; (*c*) Singers; (*d*) Headington United; (*e*) Newton Heath; and (*f*) St. Jude's Institute.
14. Which country has appeared most often in the final stages of the World Cup competition?
15. During the 1971/72 season Arsenal visited Liverpool's Anfield ground twice for a Football League match? Neither game was abandoned. What were the circumstances?
16. Below is listed a very famous England team from the past. Some of the letters in the player's names are missing. Can you fill them in, together with the missing scorers. What was the occasion?

    ENGLAND – ----- -------- 2
    Pe--rs   Ha--e-
    --r-t -   -e-e-
    ENGLAND: --n--; Co---, -ils--; S--le-,
    -h-rlt--, -oo--; Ba--, H--st,
    H--t, C-----o-, --te--.

17. Are the following statements true or false?
    (*a*) Arsenal's Scottish International goalkeeper Bob Wilson formerly played for Wolves.
    (*b*) Jimmy Greaves holds the record for the highest number of goals ever scored in Football League games.
    (*c*) Arsenal have maintained permanent membership of the First Division since gaining promotion in 1919.

71

'I'm glad the milkman called!'

(*d*) Manchester United were the first English club to play in the semi-final of the European Champions Cup.

18. Is a referee allowed to send off one of his linesmen?

19. Only one Football League club has ever won the FA Amateur Cup. Who was it?

20. Where did they play FA Cup Finals before Wembley was built?

21. Where was the first Football League Cup Final played?

22. Which club is known as 'The Shakers'?

23. When the old Fairs Cup Competition ceased in 1971, to be superseded by the EUFA Cup, what happened to the original cup?

24. What is the record score for a match in the final stages of the World Cup?

Answers on page 99

Don Revie, manager of Leeds United, may look as though he is puzzling over the answers to George Best's Quiz but he is in fact watching his team in action at Elland Road

Star quality is something Bill Shankly, manager of Liverpool, knows how to spot . . . but how did Cilla Black (No. 9 shirt too!) get in on the act? Actually, she was at Anfield to shoot a script for a television series

Confidence is a Vital Factor

by Eddie Gray

Although I suppose I am classed as one of the entertainers in football I have a great respect for the method system.

Brazil regained the World Cup by uninhibited football yet I don't believe anyone would be so foolhardy as to suggest they did so without a great deal of planning and preparation as well. They were just as much a method side as their rivals . . . but with a difference and, as the French say, *vive la difference*! All the world realized that their method was camouflaged under a fancy wrapping much more easily recognized as team-work of the highest order. The fact is that even if it includes the most talented players a team must play to a plan.

I believe most critics of the method system accept that it would be folly to go out and attempt to play a top level game simply off the cuff. What they really hate is not method teams as such, but sides which do not make their plan of campaign sufficiently flexible to allow for individual skills.

Manchester United have always been a great attraction not only at Old Trafford but wherever they have played because they have this reputation for balancing flair and method so delightfully. Likewise the fans always expect to see an exciting game whenever West Ham United are playing. Yet nobody can say that a team led by that master tactician Bobby Moore does not pay enough respect and attention to method.

I know that my own team Leeds United have been described as the arch-disciples of the method system. That might have been true at one time but which team, I ask, were the First Division's top scorers two seasons running while they were also thrilling 100,000 fans at Wembley and millions more watching that epic Wembley final on TV?

What I am leading up to is the fact that despite all the planning, all the method, all the training to get a player into peak condition, the real test is in the respective skills of two players when one has the ball at his feet and the other is confronting him.

There have always been plans to negative or at least to reduce the impact of the superior skills certain players possess. There was a time, for example, when

*Turn on the music and dance! Mick Jones (Leeds) and Phil Parkes (Wolves 'keeper)
become airborne at Elland Road*

Leeds used to send Paul Reaney out with orders to stick like a shadow to George Best whenever we played Manchester United. We were not doing anything new or unique. I am told that Sir Stanley Matthews also had to deal with this VIP treatment. Most opposing clubs used to detail one of their players just to stay has loads of confidence in his own ability and talent. He makes it look as though he is arrogant once he gets out on the park and into his stride. That is his game and the same applies to all the great ball players.

Billy Bremner, our skipper at Leeds, is another of these almost impudent players once they are in pos-

A sign of confidence. Jack Charlton's white shirt is the only sign of Leeds in this attack on the Juventus goal during the Fairs Cup Final in May, 1971

right with the famous winger. Yet the great Stan had the skills to be effective even with a personal watch-dog snapping at his heels and the point I am making is that he *knew* those skills would triumph.

Quite a few leading players of the present day can be seen parading their skills with the same assurance. Undoubtedly the prime example is George Best. He

session and demonstrating their skills. Billy oozes with confidence and he uses it to entertain the crowds. With all due modesty that is just what I try to do myself – to entertain and to play effective football. That is what we are paid to do and what the crowds come to see.

Of course there are times when our little tricks do

not come off. Sometimes our judgement is at fault and also you must not forget that there are quite a few defenders who just know they can out-think and out-manoeuvre almost any attacker. Crowds can be very unkind when you come off worst in these battles of wits and skills but if you don't have the confidence to put your skills to the test it is an awful waste of talent.

in the first place or cut off the path to goal you might have taken.

Natural skills, however, are essential if your team is going to get goals and that is what the game is all about. Even under the method system you just can't do without flair. Producing something different, a move the other side does not expect, is the only way

Terry Cooper (Leeds) and Francis Lee (Manchester City) in a race for the ball

Peter Osgood is another of these exciting players and so is Jimmy Johnstone. The big temptation to avoid is getting so carried away by the sheer thrill of beating your man that you feel you must turn back and do it all over again. That is where method, or discipline, comes in. You cannot afford to waste talent and effort like this because by the time you have done your encore the opposing defence has had time to recover and shut off the pass you should have made

goals are scored. If nobody made a mistake there would be no goals. The unexpected is the best way to bring about those mistakes by defenders.

As I say, Leeds had this reputation for being a method side. How did they grow out of it? The answer is that although individual players in the side always had confidence in their ability it needed time for that conviction to spread throughout the entire team. It was the old story of success breeding success. That was how team confidence was built up. You don't need me to tell you the result of all that. Leeds are the side all the others know they have to beat if they are going to win a competition.

But when I came to Leeds they were in the Second Division. That is a very hard division from which to win promotion. The team always had ability and

Scotland when I played for Glasgow schoolboys and then for the national schoolboys team. But I would never have qualified for the benefit of that coaching if I had not had natural ability in the first place. I developed that simply by playing as often as I could. My younger brother Frankie, now with me at Leeds, graduated the same way. I played football every spare

Joe Jordan of Leeds outjumps a Manchester United defender

individual confidence but the need to secure the right results inevitably had a restricting influence in those early days. The more success you get the more open you can be in your style of play and you create more chances. This certainly has been the case with Leeds in the last few years.

I learned a lot from the coaching I got back home in

moment I could get and there were plenty of them because there was not much else for us to do.

But when I came down to Leeds at the age of fifteen I tended to be lackadaisical. The game was played a bit different down here even at that level. It was a bit quicker and there was a wee bit more know-how. Then I had a thigh injury when I was sixteen and that kept me out of the game for a year. I played only one game in twelve months and that was a big blow, believe me.

New Year's Day is always a great occasion for any Scotsman but it was something special for me in 1966. That was the day I celebrated my début for Leeds with a goal against Sheffield Wednesday at Elland Road. Jim Storrie, a fellow Scot, gave me the pass and from twenty-five yards I shot past Ron Springett. Despite that wonderful start to my first-team career I lacked a bit of confidence for quite a while after that. I suppose I was a trifle over-awed at playing in the same team as Billy Bremner, Jack Charlton and Johnny Giles. They were all such vastly experienced players although, oddly enough, it was not until I had played with them for a while that it began to worry me. I was probably too young to think about it when I first came into the team but I found it quite a problem later on.

I can't really pinpoint the stage at which I acquired my confidence. I have been told, however, that I began to look a different player after we had played a Fairs Cup-tie in Naples. That was a rough night. It was a case of having to speed up or get caught by some of those crunching Italian tackles.

Soon after that I got my first Scotland cap and played at Wembley against the 'auld enemy'. The next time I went to Wembley I came away with the man-of-the-match award after the 1970 FA Cup Final that went to a replay. I was delighted because it was something to keep for the rest of my life but after Chelsea had taken the Cup with them from Old Trafford I would gladly have swapped my award for a winners' medal. Playing with a successful side is the main thing in acquiring confidence. It encourages you to become cheeky in a soccer sense . . . using your ability and expressing it.

Obviously we are encouraged to express ourselves at Leeds. We play open football because we think we can beat most teams whether we are playing at home or away. So even when we play away we go out to attack the other team. But if a team is not doing well an individual's confidence must suffer. If other players are not winning the ball you are struggling. You can't express your skills unless you get a good service of the ball.

To all young players I say that if you have the ability and the confidence you will do well. I have learned that confidence is vital. You must, of course, work hard at the game and train hard because your talents will be no good otherwise. If you can't run you can't play. It is as simple as that.

Shamrock Stars

by George Best

Derek Dougan, an Irishman who has played for several clubs in a number of divisions, since first joining the ranks of the professional footballers, added another aspect to a varied but distinguished career when he was elected, a year or so back, as chairman of the professional players' own union, the PFA.

Now that organization, the Professional Footballers' Association to give it its full name, is a set-up with a fine reputation within the world of soccer. Admirably led on the administrative side by its loyal and highly efficient secretary, Mr Cliff Lloyd, the PFA has always sought to have as its senior 'playing' official a man to match the post.

Although there might, at one time, have been some folk who, remembering 'The Doog' in his Cheyenne haircut days, wondered about his chairmanship of the Association, however there were never any doubts either from those who have known him well all his life or closely in recent years. For Derek Dougan, a player who often seemed to take a somewhat amused attitude on the pitch, has always been, in fact, not only deadly serious about his role ·as an entertainer,

but a remarkably fine football performer as well.

Many has been the time in conversations about the game that I have heard someone say 'Well of course, the player I reckon the most under-rated is . . .' and almost every time, before they have a chance to continue, I have been able to complete the sentence for them – by the simple statement of . . . 'Derek Dougan'.

This has not been so true in recent seasons. Maybe it is the screening of some exceptionally fine performances of his during the last few Home International Championships; or the manner in which he has come back to the 'Big Time' after being with Peterborough United, which of these two it is or could be I know not.

But one thing's for sure. The world of football and its fans really do appreciate the many, diverse talents of Derek Dougan.

So we all know his ability as a player, the magnificent performances that he has given for both his clubs and for his country, but few outside the game know how well he is doing his job as chairman of our own Association.

81

'Derek Dougan, an Irishman who has played for several clubs in a number of divisions . . . was elected, a year or so back, as chairman of the professional players' own union, the PFA'

I mentioned earlier Mr Cliff Lloyd, our wonderful secretary. The other day I heard him mention that The Doog measured up to the men who had gone before in the PFA chair, and that's certainly some predecessors in the chair were Terry Neill and Noel Cantwell.

Terry, of course, went on from that office, and from being a player with Arsenal, to become manager of

Derek Dougan (Wolves) keeps his eye on the ball as Gary Sprake (Leeds) clears his lines

tribute when you consider the previous occupants of the post, both as the PFA and before that as the Players' Union.

Talking – or should it be writing? – of the chairmen that have gone before, one does not need a particularly long memory to recall that two of Derek's immediate Hull City while Noel went from being a player and from being a chairman of the Association to become manager of Coventry City. And, of course, both have something in common with Derek. All are Irishmen!

I made this point some time ago to a friend when we were discussing Ireland's contribution to the British

83

IF YOU'LL EXCUSE AN EXPRESSION I USE . . . Above: *Blackpool's Tony Green and Millwall's Brian Brown clash in mid-field.* Right: *Luton goalkeeper Read takes a ride on the back of Millwall's Harry Cripps*

sporting scene. Nothing unfriendly about the discussion mind you, indeed it became somewhat embarrassing when we started to tot up what you might call the Shamrock Stars, past and present, in British football.

Indeed the difficulty is knowing where to start if one ever attempts to evaluate Ireland's contribution to the international sporting scene. I mean, just cast your eyes down the list of former top players who have become successful managers.

I suppose the start of a season is as good a time as any on which to make any such assessment, so in writing this I've gone back to the start of last season, and looked down the list of club managers and senior officials from my native Isle.

I have not the space to mention them all, just let us be content with lifting a small fold of the curtain as it were, and bring your attention to the Irish managers connected with my own club of Manchester United.

The present boss, Frank O'Farrell, comes to mind straight away and in the past playing category you have Noel at Coventry of course, along with Harry Gregg at Shrewsbury, Shay Brennan, managing in Ireland to, as they say, 'mention but a few'.

Of course if you delve into the past there is a fascinating panorama of great names and contributors to the game. Any person with any idea of football will recall players such as Peter Doherty, still active on the managerial side, Billy Bingham who went off to take over the Greek national side last summer; the Blanchflower brothers of Danny and Jackie; Johnny Crossan of Sunderland, Manchester City and Middlesbrough fame, not to mention that spell with Sparta of Rotterdam; Willie Cunningham of St. Mirren, Johnny Carey of Manchester United.

Wilbur Cush of Glentoran and Leeds, Alex Elder of Stoke and Burnley, and that's only up to the fifth letter of the alphabet, and with many missed out. Yes indeed, the Shamrock Stars have indeed made a massive contribution to the game.

I suppose that any fathers reading this list will be sure to disagree with me about leaving someone out, but again that makes my point even more obvious. The list is limited only by space.

The story continues today. In recent seasons I believe it is fair to say that we have not had the best of luck in the international arena. Certainly there were those in the stands, the press boxes and among the

game's managers, who felt that both in 1971 and in 1970 Ireland might, with a little more good fortune, have carried of the Home Championship Trophy.

If we had done so this would have been no fluke, no mere twist of Lady Luck's wheel in our direction. From first to last we played well in almost all our international fixtures and if there was the occasional exception it could be excused. Overall, we showed, I suggest, that as in days of yore, so today, Ireland continues to produce some fair old footballing entertainers.

I recall how at the start of last season one of our national newspapers kicked off the new session with a series on players they termed 'The Crowd-pullers'. The name is self-explanatory, and the interesting thing for me was that if it was players who give entertainment they were looking for then they went to the right folk.

I remember they started with Steve Heighway, the Liverpool forward who has earned a double Bachelor of Science degree which has his colleagues calling him 'Big Bamber', after the University Challenge chairman on television.

Well, Steve was born in Dublin, although he is of English parents. He has a great love for the place, and plays for Eire. Another they used was Nobby Stiles, who may be as English as they come but who has an Irish wife and relations, so some of the shamrock must have rubbed off on him. I was featured as well and I know that other Irish born players could have been used had not the space run out.

You get the message I hope. That whether you're Irish by parentage, by birth, or just have a bit of our blood in the family then it's odds on you'll be all the more interesting and entertaining because of it. Some have said that it is in our nature, for we Irish to wish to go on a bit, to act a bit, as if we enjoy the limelight. There could be something in that, I suppose. Anyway, one way or another, we've certainly produced some fine characters across the British scene.

Funny really but I remember the first Saturday's football of last season. I glanced at the match reports the following morning and although I'll spare any blushes by not mentioning names, out of the first three match reports I read an Irishman had on two occasions given away important goals. Well, if you can't win them all at least you can keep half the fans around the field happy.

Against that, I know that over any season in the game the Irishmen within it, whether as players, coaches, managers or what have you will have contributed far more than most, will certainly have put in much more than they can ever take out, and will fully live up to my name for them – the Shamrock Stars of Soccer.

George Best blasts a shot towards the Crystal Palace goal

'It's All Happening To Me Now'
Says MARTIN CHIVERS

by Peter Jones

The Swiss called him 'The Mighty Alp'. Everton boss Harry Catterick dubbed him 'The New John Charles'. Most experts rate him the best all-round centre-forward in Britain – and one of the best in the world. He is Martin Chivers, of course. The tall Southampton-born goal-mine who had to fight every inch of the way to get to the top – not least getting over a dreadful knee-cap injury that could easily have ended his career.

He's got the lot. Height, weight, skill, courage, split-second timing. But there was a time when Martin Chivers looked like being one of the costliest flops in soccer history.

Proving himself, at top level, meant he had to find one more quality – self-confidence. And that has led to him being unfairly dubbed a big-head, a super-ego . . . and other things even less complimentary.

So listen to Martin as he explains. 'To make the grade in what has to be the most competitive League in the world, you've got to believe in yourself. There are opponents who will do what they can to make you have doubts in yourself – therefore the only way to beat them is to have consistent confidence in your own ability to do them down.

'Once our manager at Tottenham Hotspur, Mr Nicholson, hinted that I was a bit too cocky – and therefore hadn't played up to my full form.

'Well, obviously a lot of fans assumed that I was getting too big for my boots. I'd been out of the game injured, came back and found I could still knock the goals in . . . and now it seemed that I felt I was a bit above it all. But it wasn't being big-time. It was just showing that confidence I had in my ability to dominate up front – to take on opponents and beat them by a mixture of skill and strength.

'You're nothing without that confidence. What with one thing and another, I was twenty-six before I even got into the big-time. I mean, the REAL big-time – in a successful side at White Hart Lane and in Sir Alf Ramsey's reckoning as the England number nine.

'Okay, so I'd cost Spurs about £125,000 when I joined them from Southampton. I'd won seventeen caps as an Under-23 international – and I believe that is still the record number at that level. But the Spurs

88

Martin Chivers in full action for Spurs

Martin Chivers characteristically takes to the air for England against Malta

supporters expected a lot from me – as they were entitled to at that sort of money – but it took ages for me to start doing my job, which is getting goals.

'My confidence had generally been sound, but it was badly dented when I realized I wasn't coming up with the goods as far as those supporters were concerned. Then came the real crunch. That bad injury in a game against Nottingham Forest in 1968. It's easy to get over-dramatic over these things, but the fact is that it was pretty well a miracle that I was able to play this game of soccer again.

'I'd always been a bit of a worrier. I always had this fear that I wasn't playing as consistently as I wanted. So when I did come back, and tried out that patched-up knee, I needed an extra helping of self-confidence. I did it all quite deliberately. I decided I had to show that I could go on playing – and that, I suppose, is when the talk about me being a big-head all started. There was all the transfer gossip – suggestions that Spurs might let me go if they could only find a more consistent goal-getter. That sort of talk meant I had to dig even deeper in search of confidence to bolster up what was really an inferiority complex.

'But, of course, it's all happening for me now. Spurs are really clicking as a fighting force – and I've really got the taste for international football. It's only when you have to live through an injury like that one of mine, only then that you realize what is at stake. I'd been a footballer all my working life. It was my trade.

'Anyway, the real turning-point was when I picked up about fifty goals in just twelve months. But even now I can look back on a career that had as many downs as ups – and that old Chivers' complex is still there. I mean, Southampton weren't at first particularly interested in me – mine wasn't the fairy-tale jump from school soccer to the big-time.

'And I can assure you I know only too well that my first full game for England, against Malta, was not exactly the schoolboy-story success. If I'd been left out for the rest of that year, I couldn't have complained. Instead Sir Alf showed that he had confidence in me . . . and that helped build my own confidence.'

Ask Martin's team-mates and they will assure you that he is far from being a big-head. They know, at close hand, all the pressures that go with being described as the best striker in Europe and so on. They know how upset Martin gets if he fails to score a goal – in any game, any time.

Ask Martin himself and he'll say that he feels he has a weakness in going for the far-post crosses. He reckons his timing is at fault then, though the near-post cross

Martin Chivers shows his long throw technique

he finds easy enough to gobble up. So . . . best striker in Europe or not, he spends a lot of time practising getting up to the far-post ball. He's got the speed and the strength. He knows that he is hard to dispossess, realizes that there is always a danger that he will overuse his skill on the ball – and so give the impression that he's greedy or selfish.

Realizing where the possible weaknesses are . . . that's the attribute of a realist, not a big-head.

There was one League goal against Stoke in 1970 that somehow summed up the whole magic of Martin Chivers. He picked up the ball from a tackle out on the touchline, nipped away from a defender at tremendous speed, drew out Gordon Banks no less – and delicately placed the ball past him. A virtuoso goal, wonderful to watch and supremely satisfying to the player.

Ask John McGrath, strong man of that Southampton defence, about Martin and he'll say: 'It all adds up to confidence. After that injury, Martin realized he had to give it all he'd got. Result was that he came back a much different player. Still the old skills, but a different man within himself. You can say it's cockiness if you like, but that's merely a choice of words. All I know is that he's almost impossible to play against these days because he has learned to believe in his own ability.'

Though Martin now simply won't even think about the possibility of another bad injury, fact is that he once studied to become an accountant – and maybe that accounts for the mental alertness he shows out on the park. His dad was a stevedore, in Southampton docks, and he says: 'Dad's life, and his pay-packet, taught me early on that no professional footballer should ever complain about his conditions. Playing this game is part physical and part mental. Every time the whistle goes to start a game, you're at a personal moment of truth.

'Now things are really happening for me, I can afford to think about what might have been. But it doesn't do to brood on anything in life. You have to keep looking ahead . . . finding some new ambition. I thought my one ambition was to get a full England cap, but once I got established in the team I realized there were so many other records to go for.

'Whether I'll reach them all will be a matter of luck. But at least I'm delighted that people have forgotten that big transfer fee round my neck – and accepted me in the job I can do best.'

This super-striker, astonishingly mobile for just a big chap, has always enjoyed playing in European football – with Spurs or England because he finds the defenders generally are not so physical. The back of his legs are badly scarred from the kicking he has had in English football . . . certainly prior to that 'referees' revolution' back in 1971.

And now he says: 'Though there are some players who ham it up a bit, pretend they are badly injured when they're not, the fact is that I feel desperately sorry for any player who does get a bad knock. Sometimes the worst injuries look the least worrying – and vice versa. But I know from first-hand knowledge just how hard it is to get back into the game after a long lay-off. I know how hard it is to rebuild confidence – to get rid of thoughts that it could so easily happen again. I feel sick at heart when I hear of a player getting a broken leg or something like that. It's a very long haul back.'

So . . . it really IS happening for the patient Martin Chivers now. His skill and his confidence have made him feared throughout world footballing circles. The Spurs' fans idolize him. They have realized the essential difference between self-confidence and big-headedness.

It's a pity the few Chivers knockers haven't learned the lesson. Or realized that it took a tragic injury to make him the super-confident man he is today.

Derby's Hector outjumps Everton's Keith Newton to head goalwards

Alan Ball, transferred to Arsenal from Everton for a fee in excess of £200,000

Man On The Spot

by ALAN BALL

One of the questions people often ask me, when the conversation – inevitably! – gets around to soccer is this: 'Does it worry you, when you've got to take a penalty?' And the short and simple answer to that question is . . . not really.

Every team in the country has its recognized penalty takers – the men who, at some time or other during the course of a season, are the men on the spot. For that's exactly the situation when you're called upon to take a spot-kick.

I know that Stoke and England goalkeeper Gordon Banks reckons the 'keeper should have no chance, really, when he's facing a penalty expert. It's a dead-ball situation, with the spot-kick expert having all the advantage.

He alone knows where he's intending to put the ball and the goalkeeper, admittedly, has very little time in which to make his decision. In the twinkling of an eye, the ball has been booted from the penalty spot, and even as it's travelling – maybe like a rocket – the goalkeeper has to decide and move in one swift reflex action.

In theory, the goalkeeper should always be beaten.

The penalty-taker should never miss. But, of course, it isn't always as simple as that. Many people have said, on many occasions, that football is a funny game. I'll say, with feeling, that this is an understatement.

I was one of the recognized spot-kick experts at Everton. In my footballing career, I've taken something like forty penalties, and I've scored from most of them. And some of those I've missed should have counted. For instance, I can remember a game against Chelsea, when I sent in a shot from the penalty spot which would – and should – have been a certain goal, but to this day, I have maintained that goalkeeper Peter Bonetti moved before the ball was struck. Good luck to Peter; he guessed right, and flung himself across the goal to make an amazing save. Yet, as I say, I'm convinced that as I ran up to take the kick, from the corner of my eye I saw him start to go.

Like me, you'll be too young to remember that dramatic, last-minute penalty which George Mutch scored for Preston North End against Huddersfield Town in the 1938 FA Cup Final at Wembley. It gave Preston – the team now managed by my Dad – the FA Cup. It must have been terribly nerve-wracking for every one of the players – especially Mutch – and the huge crowd.

I think, under those circumstances, ANYONE would be tense. The man taking the spot-kick, and the goalkeeper whose job it is to try to save it. We had something like that a couple of seasons ago, at Goodison Park.

Perhaps you remember, the season after we had won the First Division championship, and we played against a German team called Borussia Moenchen Gladbach in the European Cup. After our first-leg tie in Germany, and the return game at Goodison, the aggregate score was level. That meant the game had to be decided on penalties.

Of course, you could have heard a pin drop on the ground, as the players went up to take the penalty kicks. They tell me there was almost as much tension in a certain aircraft, thousands of feet up, as Liverpool were winging their way back from a European tie abroad. There was a buzz of excitement through the plane, as the captain passed the news back about the drama being enacted at Goodison . . . and everyone, apparently, was a bit keyed up until the final score became known.

Out of the five penalties each side had to take, Everton missed one, and the West German side missed two. We got through by 4–3. We had a couple of heroes, that night – Sandy Brown and goalkeeper Andy Rankin. Sandy was the man who slotted home the last of our spot-kicks, and Andy was the man who stopped the Germans in their tracks.

What do you do, when you're taking a penalty? So far as I'm concerned, I try to place the ball. I calculate that I'm the master of the situation, in so far as it's a set-piece, and the element of surprise is on my side. It's up to me to be accurate with my kick, and the ball should do the rest.

Usually, as I have said, this tactic has worked well for me, and because I've placed the ball accurately, even though the 'keeper has dived to the right side, he's been beaten because split seconds were against him. But not all players adopt the method I employ.

Big Joe Royle, for example, believes in really blasting the ball for goal. Joe's theory is simple: if he doesn't know where he's going to place the ball, what chance has the goalkeeper got? For him, it's a case of 'Guess which way I'm going'. Joe really clouts the ball and,

as he's a strapping six-footer who packs a tremendously powerful shot, you will realize that a goalkeeper might be in danger of having his head knocked off, should it get in the way of the ball.

The way Joe hammers the ball, it doesn't really matter if the goalkeeper gets his hand to it – the sheer power and pace of the shot will simply bend his hand backwards, and the ball will still rifle into the net, like a bullet from a gun. The one thing you have to be wary about, of course, is that the shot might not be quite on target. But it's a risk you take.

Johnny Morrissey is another player who has been deputed to take vital spot-kicks for Everton. A few seasons ago, when we went to the FA Cup Final against West Brom, we met and beat Leeds United in the semi-final at Old Trafford. And that game was won and lost on a penalty goal.

When the spot-kick was awarded, there was a significant pause. I was sitting that game out, through suspension, otherwise probably I'd have been handed the job. As it was, Joe Royle looked like being saddled with the business of putting the ball past Gary Sprake . . . but Joe, understandably, was nervous and hesitant about taking the kick, and Johnny took the responsibility upon his shoulders. He scored and it was the only goal of the game.

And mention of Leeds United reminds me that Johnny Giles, their little Irish international midfield star, is also a bit of an expert when it comes to tucking away a penalty. Johnny is one of the most accurate kickers of the ball in soccer, and he can chip a pass right on to the head of a team-mate. This ability has brought Leeds some goals, through the past few seasons – another little fellow called Billy Bremner has profited more than once, from those neat and precise chips of Johnny's.

It was funny how Johnny got the job of taking spot-kicks for Leeds. Bobby Collins, who played such a great part in United's revival, was the recognized penalty-taker . . . and then he missed a couple from the spot. The responsibility was passed on to Billy Bremner and he missed one. So it went to left-back Willie Bell and he failed to slot one home. Next on the list was Johnny Giles.

The first time Johnny had to take a penalty was against Birmingham, at Elland Road. He had never really practised taking penalties, but up he stepped, and

96

Alan Ball in action during his Everton days, well policed by Billy Bremner of Leeds United

used the same method that I employ. Johnny made up his mind where he was going to put the ball – in other words, he placed his shot – and he plonked it neatly past the 'keeper. He has followed the same rule ever since . . . and when I tell you that he has missed fewer than half a dozen times, from almost fifty spot-kicks, you'll agree that his way has much to commend it.

He, too, was the man right on the spot, on one occasion just as Sandy Brown, who is now with Shrewsbury, was the key man for Everton in that European Cup-tie against Moenchen Gladbach. It happened when Leeds United were playing Sunderland in an FA Cup-tie.

Leeds and Sunderland had already tangled at Elland Road and at Roker Park, and they still hadn't been able to reach a decision. So they were paired to play again, this time at Boothferry Park, the home of Hull City.

Once more, it looked as if the game was going to end as a marathon tie, because there were only a couple of minutes to go, when Jimmy Greenhoff was floored, in the penalty-box. Johnny Giles was the man on the spot, but he kept his nerve and slotted the ball home, to take Leeds into the sixth round of the cup.

If you don't remember that match, you'll probably recall Stoke's semi-final against Arsenal, last year, when the Gunners pulled a replay out of the bag with a dramatic, late equalizer. The man who picked the ball out of the net was my England team-mate, Gordon Banks . . . which just about brings me back to where I came in.

Gordon still hasn't forgotten the spot-kick Eusebio put past him in England's 1966 World Cup semi-final against Portugal. It was the first goal Gordon had conceded in the competition.

We all knew that Eusebio placed his spot-kicks to one side of the goal, and when Portugal were awarded a penalty, we signalled to Gordon, to remind him of this. One of Eusebio's team-mates saw our signals, and quickly said something to Eusebio. Gordon decided that, as Eusebio had been warned, he would place the ball in the opposite corner – so the England goalkeeper decided to dive that way. He guessed wrong . . . Eusebio did as he always did, and the ball went into the net.

So even when you're the world's greatest goalkeeper, you can't win 'em all. And as for missing the odd penalty, I think the same ruling applies there, as well.

LAWS OF PLAY 6

A goalkeeper is injured and wishes to change places with another player. Is this permitted?

(See page 106 for answer)

George Best's Soccer Quiz Answers

1. Tony Hateley. Chelsea paid Aston Villa £100,000 in October, 1966.
2. Three. Northampton, Coventry and Crystal Palace.
3. Birmingham City, who met Barcelona in the 1960 Final of the Inter-Cities Fairs Cup, now known as the EUFA Cup.
4. (a) Aberdeen; (b) Huddersfield Town; (c) Birmingham City; (d) Kilmarnock; (e) Orient; and (f) Oldham.
5. In Greece they award three points for a win, two for a draw, and one for a defeat.
6. Nottingham Forest.
7. (a) Chester; (b) Bradford Park Avenue; (c) Portsmouth; (d) Leeds United; (e) Bury; and (f) Fulham.
8. The first club to win three Championships in a row was Huddersfield Town (1924, 1925 and 1926) and the first League–Cup double was performed by Preston in 1889.
9. Trick question! *All* winners of the Scottish Cup are non-English. They are Scottish.
10. It is very rare for a club to complete its programme without a draw. The last case was back in 1896/97 when all Darwen's thirty Second Division games ended in a definite result.
11. Denis Law scored six for Manchester City in an abandoned tie against Luton in 1961 and Ted MacDougall (Bournemouth) scored six against Oxford City in 1970. A year later MacDougall scored nine against Margate!
12. The Valley, at Charlton, is the biggest League ground in England. It holds more than 70,000 spectators.
13. (a) West Ham; (b) Stockport County; (c) Coventry City; (d) Oxford United; (e) Manchester United; and (f) Queen's Park Rangers.
14. Brazil have appeared in the final stages of all nine World Cup competitions to date – the only country with a 100 per cent record.
15. Arsenal first played at Anfield against Manchester United when Old Trafford had been closed by the FA because of crowd disturbances. Arsenal later returned to Anfield to fulfil their normal fixture with Liverpool.
16. The occasion was, of course, the 1966 World Cup Final. Here are the details in full:

ENGLAND 4	WEST GERMANY 2
Peters	Haller
Hurst 3	Weber

    ENGLAND: Banks; Cohen, Wilson; Stiles, Charlton, Moore; Ball, Hurst, Hunt, Charlton, Peters.
17. (a) True. Wilson was once a Wolves' amateur.
    (b) False. Greaves holds the record for First Division games; Arthur Rowley's record of 434 for all League games still stands.
    (c) False. Arsenal were *elected* to the First Division in 1919. They did not win promotion.
    (d) True. United first appeared in the semi-final in 1957.
18. Yes. If the linesman is not performing his duties properly the referee can dismiss him.
19. Middlesbrough.
20. The last final before Wembley was opened in 1923 was played at Chelsea. FA Cup Finals have also been staged at Lillie Bridge (London), The Oval, Derby, Everton, Fallowfield (Manchester), Bolton, Crystal Palace, Bramall Lane and Old Trafford.
21. The first final in 1961 was played on a home and away basis between Aston Villa and Rotherham.
22. Bury.
23. A challenge match, to decide permanent ownership of the Fairs Cup, was staged between Barcelona and Leeds United in Spain in 1971. Barcelona won 2–1.
24. Hungary 9, Korea 0 in 1954.

TEAM SPIRIT

by TOMMY SMITH

Team spirit is the one thing that money cannot buy in football. You can spend a lot of money signing a player who possesses terrific skill – he may be a great winger, a scoring striker, a wonderful midfield player or a strong back-four defender. But if he doesn't fit into the picture, a lot of that cash will have been wasted.

I cannot talk about any club other than Liverpool; because I have known no other club, ever since I became a professional footballer. But this I do know: all the teams which are in the running for honours possess team spirit . . . if they didn't, they wouldn't be successful. As for Liverpool, our record speaks for itself – and for the team spirit which really does exist at Anfield.

It was Sir Matt Busby who said, several years ago, that if things are right at the top, they'll be right further down the line. That's true. At Anfield, we have a team behind the team – and the members of it play a vital role in the success of the side which takes the field.

Manager Bill Shankly, his assistant, Bob Paisley, Reuben Bennett, Geoff Twentyman, Ronnie Moran,

Joe Fagan, Tom Saunders. All these men dovetail together, in the various roles they play, whether it's planning for the first team, scouting for new talent, handling the reserves and the juniors or attending to the needs of the youngsters trying to break through. That's the job Tom Saunders does, for instance – he's Liverpool's Youth Development Officer.

Bob Paisley, like others in this off-the-field team, served Liverpool as a player. He helped them to reach Wembley in 1950; he was trainer in 1965 and last year, when we reached the final of the FA Cup. Bob's long service means loyalty – and the same can be said about many members of our backroom team.

Now what about Bill Shankly, the manager? – Well, everyone knows a great deal about him . . . but the people who work with him and play for him know 'the boss' better than most. His record speaks for itself, in the decade that he's been the manager. Two league championships, two FA Cup Finals – and the 1965 Final was the first time that Liverpool had ever won the trophy.

Wherever people talk soccer, they tell 'Bill Shankly stories'. What 'the boss' said or did, on a certain

'I beg your pardon!'
Expressions say much in
this Rangers v. *Celtic clash*

Bill Shankly, manager of Liverpool, in vocal mood at Anfield

102

occasion. And, of course, the stories often improve with the telling. But the main thing about Liverpool's manager is his unswerving faith in his club and his team, no matter what. He has that wonderful ability to inspire players with his own, fervent belief. Don't take my word for it; just ask ANY of the Liverpool players, and they will confirm what I say.

When you're up against it, 'the boss' will find the right words to take away that nervous tension. Not just that; he'll find the words which inspire you to walk out feeling ten feet tall . . . feeling, in fact, that you cannot help but beat the opposition, because you KNOW you're better than your individual opponent, and a better team than the opposition, collectively. Oh, 'the boss' can hammer you, all right, when he thinks you need it. But, always, the effect is good for you – and for the team.

When Liverpool played Leeds and won the FA Cup at Wembley in 1965, I was a comparative new boy. Names like Lawrence, Lawler, Byrne, Stevenson, Yeats, Strong, Callaghan, Hunt, St. John and Thompson were automatic on the team sheet, and I wore the unfamiliar No. 10 jersey. Little did I dream that when the 1971 Cup Final came round, I would be the skipper who led the team out at Wembley.

Ron Yeats, who had received the Cup at the end of the 1965 Final, was a spectator in 1971 – he was sitting it out, watching from the line, along with the manager and the backroom staff. But big Ron was willing us to win just as much as if he had been out there on the Wembley turf.

Let me tell you of an incident which happened almost two years ago, when we were flying back from a European tie. Big Ron, who had gone on the trip, suddenly appeared at the head of the plane, to announce himself over the loudspeaker system. 'Gentlemen, this is your ex-captain speaking . . .' That was how he began. Then he went on to act as the compere of an impromptu concert, and he had various people, including players, directors and pressmen, going up to the mike to do a turn. He even got 'the boss' up there, to say his piece. The hours passed swiftly, and almost before we knew it, we were touching down at Speke airport. Ronnie Yeats, Liverpool's ex-captain, had played a part off the field in cementing the tremendous team spirit which already existed at the club. And his loyalty to Liverpool was rewarded, little more than a year ago, with a new contract.

LAWS OF PLAY 7

BALL LEAVES
PLAY HERE

*Is it in order to take a quick throw-in from behind the touch-line opposite
to the point where it left play?*

(See page 106 for answer)

That's just one example of how team spirit is forged and strengthened by the attitude people inside a club adopt. I will never forget, too, how we overcame the very real handicap of injuries in the 1970–71 season. For a start, there had been quite a bit of team rebuilding. Ray Clemence, Alec Lindsay and Larry Lloyd had come into the defence. I was the new skipper. I

Just when it seemed our defence was doing far better than we had the right to expect, our attack was thrown into confusion by those injuries, and we were having to start all over again.

Even the greatest optimists at Anfield were not prepared to predict quick success for Liverpool, just then. But what happened? – Everyone pitched in to

Steve Heighway celebrates Liverpool's opening goal as Peter Thompson (No. 12) runs to congratulate him. FA Cup Final, 1971

have to admit that I anticipated it would take us all at least a season to settle down and really get to know each other's style of play, for there were several new faces in the side at once.

Then it happened – almost overnight, it seemed, players like Ian Callaghan, Alun Evans, Bobby Graham and Peter Thompson were struck down by injuries which put them out of action for months, never mind weeks. New and inexperienced players were flung into the front line – names like Brian Hall, Steve Heighway, Phil Boersma began to be known.

help everyone else; experienced players covered for those who lacked experience; in fact, there wasn't a man who gave less than one hundred per cent – and we all tried to give more!

At the end of the season, we were sadly contemplating the fact that we hadn't managed to win the FA Cup, or the European Fairs Cup. But we HAD reached the FA Cup Final, we HAD reached the semi-finals of the European Fairs Cup, and we DID finish fifth in the League – and remember that the First Division is the hardest League in the world to win.

104

What was more, we had equalled the club's own record by having conceded only 24 goals in 42 League games.

Our efforts had shown that we had tremendous strength in depth, especially when it was remembered that the reserves had won the Central League championship for the third successive season. As for Hunt and Ian St. John departed. New names, new faces became known to the Anfield faithful – and were taken to their hearts. All the time, no matter who was in the first team or who was out of it, Liverpool kept right on going. That was the measure, and still is the measure, of our tremendous team spirit.

George Graham slips in the equalizing goal for Arsenal in the FA Cup Final, 1971

the first team, the competition was greater than ever, and we were going into our eighth European campaign, this time the Cup Winners' Cup.

If I seem to be shouting the praises of Liverpool, I can claim as an excuse (not that I need one!) that our record is one which demonstrates so clearly how consistently well we have done, right through ten years at the top, since we came out of the Second Division.

The great team of the 1960s was broken up, and stalwarts like Willie Stevenson, Geoff Strong, Roger

It's something which, as I said at the start of this article, money simply cannot buy. You can have eleven talented players, but if each man is playing for himself, you will not have a TEAM. Neither will you have team spirit. But if you have players of talent who are also prepared to put everything into their game, not just for themselves, but for the sake of everyone at the club – AND for the club – then you are really on the right road to success. You simply cannot fail.

105

Team spirit . . . money cannot buy it. And it cannot be seen. But when you walk into the dressing-room, and hear the players laughing, cracking jokes, having each other on . . . then you know that the club concerned HAS got team spirit. You live by it, you live with it and from it, you gather the strength which carries you through the rough patches, and leads you to the very top.

Laws of Play (Answers)

LAWS OF PLAY

The drawings and questions in this book have been reproduced from *Association Football Laws Illustrated* (Pelham £1.50) by courtesy of the author, Stanley Lover. His book has been officially approved and recommended by the Referees' Committee of FIFA.

Sir Stanley Rous contributes a Foreword and Mr Ken Aston a Preface. As Sir Stanley says, Stan Lover's book will help the many thousands of soccer followers throughout the world to understand the Laws of the Game.

Answers to Questions

1. Yes.
2. The moment the whole of the ball has crossed the goal-line it is out of play. The game would be stopped and a goal-kick awarded to the defending team.
3. Only when an indirect free-kick is to be taken from a position less than 10 yards from the goal. Defenders may stand on the goal line between the posts.
4. No. The Referee must restart the game by dropping the ball at the place where the interference occurred.
5. No. The ball is not in play until it touches the ground. In this case the Referee would drop the ball again.
6. Yes, at any time provided that the Referee is advised when the change is to be made.
7. The ball must be thrown-in from the point where it crossed the touch-line, not as shown.

Steve Heighway (Liverpool) with Norman Hunter (Leeds) out to stop him

*Chris Lawler (Liverpool)
on duty for England*

George Best selecting the pictures to be used in this Annual

GEORGE BEST
–off the Soccer Field

George Best with Mr Mervyn Ratnor, Managing Director of Shirleys Shops, at a party launching a new range of George Best Lincroft clothes for boys

George Best takes a break during the filming of a TV commercial

George Best shows off his latest Soccer Kit Bag

The Pleasures of Playing for ENGLAND

by BOBBY MOORE

Every boy who ever kicked a football between two coats in his local park has acted out a soccer dream . . . a dream that one day he would play for England. I was no exception. But I was one of the very few lucky ones for I grew up to fulfil the greatest ambition of all by skippering England to triumph in the 1966 World Cup.

I could not have had a happier or a prouder moment. I can still hear the roar of E-N-G-L-A-N-D, E-N-G-L-A-N-D in my ears as I walked up to collect the Jules Rimet Trophy. You could almost feel the goodwill being shouted out by the Wembley crowd and the thousands more who were leaping up and down in front of their television sets at home.

Nothing could ever top the elation I felt at that moment. I was the king of the world, the captain of the all-conquering soccer nation. That was the peak of my soccer achievement to date. That moment gave me the greatest single thrill, but my long career with England has given me so many other moments of pleasure.

With England I have travelled the world, made thousands of friends, played with and against the greatest stars and earned much fame and honour. It is

a wonderful life. One of my favourite relaxations is to spend time at home with souvenirs of my travels with England that bring back so many happy memories. But despite all the cups and awards, it's always the more personal items which have meant most to me.

I'm sure you have noticed the habit players have of exchanging shirts at the end of an important game. Well, this has brought me two of the possessions I prize most of all. They are shirts worn by Pele and Eusebio, two of the greatest players in the world. I swapped shirts with Pele after our World Cup match in Guadalajara, which Brazil won by the only goal of the match. I remember saying to him as we did so: 'See you in the Final.' He replied: 'Yes, I think you will.' As you know, it did not work out like that because we were knocked out by West Germany.

Most friends who see Eusebio's shirt reckon I must have collected it after our World Cup semi-final at Wembley in 1966. Actually I received it two years earlier in Sao Paulo when I was playing for England Youth during the 'Little World Cup'.

As I write about the pleasure I receive from my

Bobby Moore leads England on to the field before an international against Scotland

111

international souvenirs I am brought back to that fabulous day when we beat West Germany to win the World Cup in 1966. Pride of place among my collection goes to the shirt I wore in that game. It is something I will never part with – and I'm certain the rest of the players feel exactly the same way.

seeing the world as an England player, and there are few countries I haven't visited. Top of my present list is Brazil, a lively and exciting country. There is always so much to see and do there – particularly at Rio de Janeiro, formerly the capital, which is set in a bay at the edge of the Atlantic.

Bobby Moore kisses the World Cup after England's victory at Wembley in 1966

In the 1966 World Cup every captain who played against Mexico was given a giant sombrero, and I collected many other gifts when we were in Mexico for the next World Cup. In fact I have quite a collection of souvenirs from all over the world. These are the links to last a life-time, and to remind me of the pleasures of a great career.

Few people can have as many opportunities of

I've played against Brazil a couple of times in Rio, but unfortunately we were beaten on both occasions. I'm offering no excuses for 1964, when we were crushed 5–1. As the score suggests, we were outplayed by the far better side on the day. But the next time, in 1969 at Rio, England were very unlucky to lose. We were well in command for most of the match and led by a Colin Bell goal, but the Brazilians put the ball

112

into the back of our net twice near the end to make it 2–1. Despite those defeats I'll never forget that fascinating city with the Sugar Loaf Mountain and the statue of Jesus overlooking the lively, teeming streets below.

Apart from the World Cup Final, three other matches have given me special pleasure. The first was playing World Champions Brazil towards the end of the 1962–63 season. It was an ambition of mine to be in a side to play them at Wembley, and I gained a lot of satisfaction from that game which we drew 1–1. Naturally, the second was when I was first appointed captain of England in the match against Czechoslovakia in Bratislava. England won the game 4–2 on May 29th, 1963. The third was England's match against the Rest of the World early in the next season. We crowned a great occasion by clinching the game 2–1. Among the men we opposed were Yashin (Russia), Santos (Brazil), Schnellinger (West Germany), Eusebio (Portugal), Di Stefano (Spain), Gento (Spain), Puskas (Hungary), and Law and Baxter (Scotland).

My England career has won me honour and a lot of fame. Wherever I go I am instantly recognized and, although this can be a strain, I enjoy the popularity and glamour. When I sit down in a restaurant there is always somebody who wants my autograph for sons and daughters and other relatives and friends.

It seems every move I make becomes headlines. Once the papers even splashed a story about me jamming my finger in my car door. I even receive letters that are simply addressed to Bobby Moore, England. That is the price of fame, but don't think I'm complaining. I love every minute of it.

If I select a team from some of the stars I have played alongside and against it is embarrassing to think of the brilliant players I must leave out. However, my team would be in 4–2–4: Banks (England); Alberto (Brazil), J. Charlton (England), Shesternev (Russia), Wilson (England); R. Charlton (England), Gerson (Brazil); Jairzinho, Pele (Brazil), Greaves (England), Best (N. Ireland).

I'm certain you would never find a better goalkeeper than Banks. I'll never forget the save he made from Pele in our match against Brazil in Guadalajara – a save Pele said was the greatest he had ever seen. I have included Alberto, skipper of Brazil in the 1970 World Cup, while Ray Wilson must be the best leftback I have encountered. Then I doubt if you could get two better stoppers than Jackie Charlton and

Bobby Moore exchanges shirts with Pele after the England v. *Brazil World Cup match in Mexico, 1970*

113

Albert Shesternev. In midfield I have chosen Bobby Charlton and Gerson. The England players were more impressed with Gerson than any other Brazilian player when we watched them beat Czechoslovakia in Guadalajara. He was injured and couldn't play against us, but after watching him in the semi-final and final I can only say he is one of the best midfield men of all time.

No superlatives can exaggerate the skills of Pele, the Black Pearl, who dazzled in Mexico before he bowed out of the international scene. Another brilliant Brazilian is Jairzinho who scored in every round of the World Cup and hit their winner against us. I could not possibly leave him out of the side.

Jimmy Greaves, who retired from the game at the end of 1970–71, was a master of taking half-chances. I was delighted that Jimmy finished his career with West Ham.

When the side is completed by the genius of George Best, it is marvellous to imagine this team playing together. A team of great individual players does not necessarily blend together into a great side. Nevertheless, it's nice to imagine – and I have the pleasure of thinking I have played with all of them.

These pleasures will live longer in my memory than the few sad moments . . . like when we were knocked out of the 1970 World Cup by West Germany. It was a sorry sight in the dressing-room. None of us could really understand what had happened, how we could have been so close to success only to have it snatched from our grasp at the last moment. I could hardly believe it – we were no longer World Champions. Two goals up with only twenty minutes to go in the quarter-final at Leon and we lost.

Our team manager, Sir Alf Ramsey, said later that our defeat was 'one of the great mysteries of football'. I could not agree more. I just cannot pin-point a reason for failure. It stands out as one of the few isolated moments of misery in a wonderful career with England.

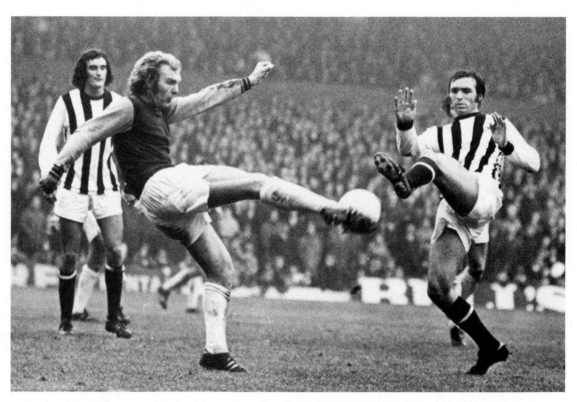

Bobby Moore (West Ham) kicks the ball clear from Jeff Astle (West Brom) during a league match

Soccer is a branch of Show Business

by TONY BLACKBURN

Sometimes I've watched Georgie Best in action, especially in those slowed-down television sequences, I've marvelled at the sheer skill of the man. I mean, he's not exactly a physical giant, but he takes on thundering great defenders and invariably makes them look a bunch of mugs.

And, if he happens to be wearing the number eight shirt, I think back to my own schooldays when I was a highly ambitious inside-right, fairly handy as a goal-scorer and thoroughly enjoying my game.

For sure, I'd never have made the grade as a professional. No chance at all of that, and anyway I had an idea then that I'd finish up in some branch of show-business. Nowadays I mix just a little soccer, mostly in charity games, with a whole lot of entertainment work.

George, of course, does it the other way round. A lot of soccer, at top business level, and maybe a little entertainment outside – say in commercials, or in small parts in movies.

Soccer and show-biz. There are some who still doubt whether there is a real link between the two. But me, I am absolutely certain that the two professions are bound together with an unloosable knot.

Actually I don't want to bore you with all the details of my soccer-playing life. It wasn't long enough to make much of an impact. We were allowed to play soccer at the prep-school where I first started grappling with reading and writing – but when I moved on to Millfield, which is a public school, the order was that we had to play Rugby football.

I'm afraid I didn't exactly shine with the oval ball. Not a bad game, mind you, but the fact is that I much preferred soccer. Long before I left school, I'd decided that I was going to find work connected with pop music. It wasn't long before I was singing with dance-bands and learning to cope with a microphone.

So . . . the end product is that I got so involved in being a disc-jockey, which means working most weekends, that I rather lost touch with soccer. I sometimes go to Chelsea, along with my manager Harold Davison, who has one of those super-plush glass-fronted boxes there, and I must say I enjoy seeing the games.

I enjoy watching the game, and the interviews, on the old goggle-box. So I keep in touch, but without

'Sometimes I've watched Georgie Best in action, especially in those slowed-down television sequences, and I've marvelled at the skill of the man'

having become one of those fanatical supporters who goes everywhere with one particular team.

And as for the playing side . . . well, I get some useful exercise out of our charity games with the BBC disc-jockeys. Mind you, there's more show-biz than soccer in those efforts, even though we pull in some very big crowds. John Peel, for instance, contributes the real soccer skill – he really is a very good player, with amazing ball control, and he also thinks deeply about the game.

Terry Wogan, too, obviously knows a bit about soccer. To enable us to put up some kind of a show, we 'import' some producers and backroom boys, but I'm afraid that the contributions of Dave Cash, John Moran and sometimes that football fanatic Pete Murray is more concerned with slapstick than soccer.

We are the ones who empty buckets of cold water over each other and generally play the fool. But then we get back to the point that soccer and show-biz really are linked together. We'd draw no crowds at all if we genuinely tried to play straight soccer, with no messing around. So charity would suffer – and probably so would I, in terms of muscle strains and so on.

Anyway, let's get back to the show-biz element in top-class soccer . . . let's stop me trying to explain why I didn't become another Derek Dougan or Alan Ball.

Take that man George Best. Everybody knows he's a world-class player, with all the talents and all the skills. But he also puts on an entertainment. I've heard that he alone can put 15,000 on a gate, and there aren't all that many pop stars who could do that.

Everything about him has that aura of the big star. He could surely have become a film-star, or a television personality or anything he wanted. Where soccer had been short on the pin-up personalities, he came along and changed the whole 'face' of the game – and I do mean 'face'.

So he's a star. Tony Curtis is a star as is Roger Moore.

Same thing goes with soccer. Players like Steve Heighway, of Liverpool, or Chelsea's Peter Osgood. Denis Law – now there's someone who, in top form, really does entertain what we call the masses.

I suppose it's harder for defenders to get that glossy show-biz aura, but Bobby Moore has managed it. He pulls the crowds, he dominates games and he's pinned up in many a fair damsel's bedroom.

And they have a following of millions. Some players,

brilliant players, don't have that aura. If you like, they are short on actual glitter. It's very much the same in pop music. Many talented singers and musicians who just don't have the personality to emerge as real stars.

But, to be honest, one thing does worry me a bit about all this. It seems to me that soccer has become an actual drug for lots of people – and I'm anti-drugs, no matter what shape they come in.

I've worked in clubs around Manchester on Saturday evenings, doing my 'live' disc-jockey work. The records go down well, but every so often you get the rival soccer fans chanting out their messages of support. It can get pretty bitter at times, and one can see how mere rivalry can easily explode into sheer violence.

So I was pleased to read that players like George Best say they have no time at all for the hooligans who go to games, armed to the teeth with weapons and seemingly determined to get involved in a fight. I'm glad that the players themselves just don't regard these fans as real supporters. Actually, they're not even fans of football.

Then there's the theory that violence on the pitch can cause violence on the terraces. Really that's another link with show-biz, because that's equally true of some of the pop groups. There are several who deliberately create a sort of riot-raising atmosphere then look very surprised when riots actually start in the audiences.

Anyway, there's no doubt at all that soccer has become very much a part of show-business. Fair enough – we can stand the competition. Mind you it's not in the same category as professional wrestling, but we should remember that there are thousands of amateur wrestlers who are in the game simply because they love it.

I don't know how much money a star like George Best gets out of the game, though I've seen several guesses. But his pay-packet is his business and anyway I doubt if it works out as much as a top show-biz star can get.

But as one of the soccer super-stars, I'll bet he gets maybe more money from the so-called fringe benefits. Like personal appearances and giving his name to various products.

And I must admit the same is true with me. I get a fair whack for my actual broadcasting, but there is more coming in from outside interests. Once you've built a bit of a name for yourself, there's no shortage of offers from outside.

To survive, soccer has to keep throwing up superstar figures, just as the entertainment scene has to do.

Sometimes I wish I had a bit more spare time to get more involved with soccer, but if that was true, then it would simply mean I wasn't doing so well in my actual job. So it's a kind of vicious circle.

I wouldn't want to change places with Georgie Best; and I'm sure he wouldn't want to change jobs with me. But, in an odd sort of way, I reckon we're linked up in the same business.

The business called entertainment!

'I wouldn't want to change places with Georgie Best; and I'm sure he wouldn't want to change jobs with me. But, in an odd sort of way, I reckon we're linked up in the same business. The business called entertainment'

Why I Chose Newcastle United

by Malcolm Mac Donald

Last year I became Soccer's costliest striker when Newcastle United forked out a staggering £180,000 for me. At the time only Martin Peters and Ralph Coates, two creators rather than scorers, had cost more. In other words, it was a big, big transfer but it took me only half an hour with Newcastle boss Joe Harvey before I signed.

For a Cockney lad who had spent all his life in the south with Tonbridge, Fulham and Luton Town it must have looked a mighty quick decision to move so far north. Footballers these days tend to dawdle over moves. Little things seem to sway their decisions and make them waver. They worry about what the area is like, if the wife will like it, and if the houses are cheap. It all seems daft to me. Football is a business like any other and such trivialities shouldn't matter. We are only in the game for a very short time and therefore I believe in getting my priorities right. When Newcastle made the plunge for me I believe I did just that.

All I wanted to know from the boss was what cash I would be getting and if I would fit into the set-up at Gallowgate. Once I was satisfied on these two points I signed. I had never seen the city and had no wish to. It didn't come into it.

The morning I left to complete the deal it was my wife Julie's twenty-first birthday. I put on a good suit, kissed her goodbye and said: 'I'll probably be home late, luv. I might be signing for a new club today.' That was it. Nothing more. She understood that this was business and I would do my best for both of us. Whatever part of the country we had to move to for a short while didn't matter. After all, I can move back to London if I want once I stop playing.

A lot of people thought I would be disappointed when I learned later that Chelsea had gone in with a late bid only to be told that I was on my way to Newcastle. On the surface I suppose Chelsea did look an ideal club for me. Their ground is only two miles from where I used to live and thirty minutes from where my wife lived. And my mother was born there. It was the perfect family set-up but really that doesn't enter into things. Sentiment cannot be allowed to cloud anyone's judgement in business.

To be absolutely frank I would have signed for

Stockport County in the Fourth Division if the money had been right and they could have convinced me I would win an England cap with them. Glamour is all very well but it won't keep me or my family. I don't mean to sound mercenary, only realistic. Football is not a sport any longer. It's a business. Newcastle put down the cash and in return they got a player who will give them his last drop of blood. From now on New-

I knew for weeks before my transfer that I was on the move. Alec Stock, Luton's manager, was very fair with me. He told me that I was doing very well and was a vital member of the team but that financially Luton would be unable to hold on to me much longer. I was scoring a lot of goals and the big boys were taking notice. Obviously Luton, who had paid their players good money in the hope of clinching pro-

Two Newcastle United favourites. Left: *Bobby Moncur and*, right, *Malcolm MacDonald*

castle United are my club. They have got my complete loyalty and whatever talent I possess, and the fact that they are a First Division club with a great tradition is a bonus.

motion to the First Division, couldn't refuse a massive offer that would balance their books.

I knew Manchester United's Sir Matt Busby had been watching me regularly and naturally I was

120

That's my ball! Ferguson (West Ham) stops Newcastle's Tudor in a league match last September

flattered. He's Mr Football to everyone in the game. But I kept a steady head. Then Joe Harvey and director Stan Seymour began turning up regularly at Kenilworth Road, so it looked as though I was bound for one of the Uniteds.

Both clubs came so often that I thought they had taken out a season ticket. But you can hardly blame them. If I was spending £180,000 I would want to know everything about the player I was getting and I mean everything. His private life, the lot. I would even consider hiring a private detective!

Manchester United had been given the first option on me but as time went on it looked more and more as though Newcastle's persistence would pay off. Manchester were undergoing a hunt for a new manager and this obviously curtailed their chance of buying as the new manager would naturally pick his own players and wouldn't want someone spending £180,000 for him, so Newcastle, with no such problems, became favourites. I didn't mind.

We wrapped up the season by beating Cardiff City and I scored a hat-trick to reach my thirty-goal target for the season. The next day I was due to play at Margate in a benefit match and I was told by Mr Stock to take it very easy and report to the ground early next morning well dressed. I hadn't to be told that it was Newcastle.

Before I left Kenilworth Road for a get-together with Joe Harvey, secretary Malcolm Hoole and Luton assistant manager Harry Haslam in a London hotel, Mr Stock phoned my agent. He arranged for everything to be kept quiet for a few hours so we would be undisturbed and then set up a Press conference. It worked like a charm. Everything went smoothly and I felt pretty pleased with myself – until I got home. Then I suddenly realized I'd forgotten to get my wife a twenty-first card! 'Never mind – I've brought you a few quid as a present,' I said, brightening. But it didn't work. 'I can't keep money in a drawer and look at it in a few year's time,' answered Julie. There was no reply to that.

I expected the First Division to be frightening. It's the élite, the best in the world and for a twenty-one-year-old the challenge was immense. But the jump hasn't been as hard as I thought. There is not so much outright clogging as there is in the Second and Third Divisions. Defenders are more subtle, more clever.

I've needed a season to adjust and to learn, of course, but I think I've done that, and I think I've shut up one or two Doubting Thomases as well. One of them said I wouldn't score fifteen goals in the top flight, but after I'd played and scored at his ground he wanted me in the England team. What's more, he said it in print. A member of a London club was another. He wrote that his team didn't rate me, but in our League game I whipped a couple of goals past him in a three-minute spell even though we lost. Mind you, I don't see myself as a wonder boy. Far from it. I know my faults better than anyone and the list's as long as my arm. My good points are few but I have two that are vital – I can run like the wind and I can put the ball in the back of the net. These days that commodity is as precious as gold, and I'm hoping it can sustain me at the top for another ten years.

If you want to play Soccer really well study

ON THE BALL

By GEORGE BEST

The helter-skelter Soccer City

by David Jones

Out of the ambiguous world of the Second Division swept Sheffield United, breaching strongholds of defensive football with a style full of daring; conjuring up for supporters of soccer everywhere images that evoked the kind of emotion we had as young children reading about the deeds of brave young knights in shining armour riding powerful white chargers to victory.

Sheffield, the city that gave organized football to the world, vividly reminded us at the start of the 1971–72 season that soccer is an entertainment – a game to excite and to enjoy. Sheffield, the helter-skelter city of football, helped to rekindle a genuine enthusiasm for the game at a time when violence and boring safety-first systems by robot-minded managers were threatening to choke it slowly to death.

Sheffield wasn't alone of course, but nowhere was the love of attacking, intuitive, inventive football stronger; nowhere were players more prepared than those at Bramall Lane to explore the wider freedom created by the clampdown on men trying to take over football by force.

On the other hand, no one outside of Bramall Lane and in his right mind would have forecast in the summer of 1971 that United were about to make the most dynamic return to the First Division in years. They clearly had the talent to succeed, but for decades Sheffield had been a soccer city without the will or imagination to challenge for the game's leadership. And having had no real achievement to cheer for years supporters had grown used to hiding their shame under dusty tales from a glorious but very distant past; or they had simply stopped caring.

Sheffield had become desperate for some of the football success lavished on the game's followers in cities like Manchester, Liverpool and Leeds; and with its two major soccer clubs lying becalmed for years, Sheffield had also steadily drifted towards the status of a second-class sporting city.

Against such a depressing background United worked guardedly towards their First Division come-back, and the most significant landmark in the build-up to their brilliant return to the top came at the start of 1971 when they signed goalkeeper John Hope, mid-field general Trevor Hockey and attacker David Ford all in one frenetic day.

Alan Woodward (Sheffield United)

On the eve of their return to the First Division, United chairman Dick Wragg looked back to that unprecedented dash into the transfer market and revealed: 'The day we went shopping and bought three players was the day United began to see the light. We mortgaged the club a bit, but the gamble paid off.'

Wragg, a visionary who has played an important part in the football fortunes of the nation as well as his native city, also forecast that if United continued to be as skilful as they had been during the previous promotion year they would have no difficulty holding their position in the First Division. Even a man prepared to gamble as much as Wragg would not have dared forecast what happened next – for only eleven days after the season began United had completed a remarkable hat-trick of victories over the champions from the three previous seasons – Leeds, Everton and 'double' winners Arsenal – and two of those successes were away from home.

One of the players told me: 'We believed in ourselves and we knew we had the ability. But to be honest after each victory over those great sides – especially that win over double champions Arsenal – we would look at each other in amazement when we got back to the dressing room.'

It was wonderful to see again huge, singing, chanting, chattering crowds enjoying their football in Sheffield –, spectators able to match boast for boast with the best in the land. John Harris, the manager who led United back with such a firm belief in attacking football, says that it is not possible to fool Sheffield fans: 'They will only accept the genuine thing. They will never be taken in by a fake.'

Harris says he felt he belonged in Sheffield the moment he arrived: 'It is a city I love. The people are straight, open and so genuine. As long as you are prepared to take them for what they are they will reciprocate. You also play football the way you live and your honesty shows in your game.'

Another momentous step in the great Sheffield football revival was the decision to ask Yorkshire County Cricket Club to leave Bramall Lane so that United could build a four-sided ground that would not retard their growing ambitions. At the start of 1971 I had organized a public debate to see what Sheffield thought about getting rid of cricket from Bramall Lane and though a wonderful discussion ended with a narrow vote in favour of keeping a dual ground I felt sure the

Sheffield United players converge on the Nottingham Forest man in possession of the ball

Alan Woodward (Sheffield United) and Steve Kember (Chelsea)

demand for progress was getting stronger all the time.

Behind the scenes another vital part of United's plan for a big new future was being put together brilliantly by their commercial manager Harold Rumsey. While carefully retaining the ground's historic fabric Rumsey installed the modern comforts and attractions needed to develop football commercially. After working for some of the country's leading clubs Rumsey decided United's potential offered the finest challenge, and like Harris believes Sheffield supporters will buy only the genuine article: 'They don't go around like they do at a lot of other clubs saying they're going to win everything, and they take a long time to make up their minds.'

Sheffield did not take long making up its mind about Tony Currie however, and with the return to the First Division the blond and brilliant athlete quickly gained the wide recognition he had long deserved. Watford had just dropped him in 1968 when United snapped him up for £27,500 and today the price on his head would be frightening to anyone. He was seventeen when he moved North, and though he still has a thick London accent he regards himself very much a Sheffielder.

Currie's great hero is Pele and many of the game's leading experts believe there is much of Pele's genius in Currie's play. Superbly built, the United youngster shields the ball very like the great Brazilian, and after bewildering changes of pace and direction he has the same happy knack as Pele of being able to look up and decide instantly to startle a goalkeeper with a fierce shot no matter what the range.

However the key to Sheffield's return to being a football power in the land is to be found in a willingness by everyone to run and help others – perhaps the vital part in the make-up of every outstanding team.

While United were chasing hard to make up for all the lost chances in Sheffield's football story, Derek Dooley, the city's great folk hero, quietly worked on recolouring the faded image of Sheffield Wednesday, and though Dooley's efforts were less spectacular than his rival's across the city they indicated firmly that Sheffield wanted to get back in the race – that in a football sense the city had again found a will to succeed.

Twenty years earlier Dooley the giant, red-headed centre-forward had blazed the name of Sheffield across the land until a tragic accident at Preston led to him losing his right leg. And when he was appointed team-manager at Hillsborough in succession to Danny Williams many suspected that the Wednesday Board – heavily under attack from disillusioned supporters – were hoping the hero-worship for Dooley would take people's minds off their own failings.

Dooley had in fact been close to applying for the job once or twice before Wednesday asked him to take over from the previous manager, and when the offer came he reckoned he could not turn it down otherwise he might have regretted it the rest of his life. He was very aware of the special way thousands adored him still for his great deeds all those years before, and he knew when he took the job that if things went wrong he could easily lose many of his friends.

He felt, however, that Wednesday supporters were entitled to success and that he was capable of giving it to them: 'I wasn't bothered about anybody saying you've done a bloody good job. I thought if I could go in there and make the team go, make it tick, I would pay something back to the game and to Wednesday.'

With that kind of spirit Sheffield can make up for all the wasted years – and not slip behind again in the chase for honours.

*Len Badger
(Sheffield United)*